1972

THE REFERENCE SHELF   VOLUME 43 NUMBER 6

WOMEN AND SOCIETY

EDITED BY
DIANA REISCHE

THE H. W. WILSON COMPANY
NEW YORK   1972

THE REFERENCE SHELF

The books in this series contain reprints of articles, excerpts from books, and addresses on current issues and social trends in the United States and other countries. There are six separately bound numbers in each volume, all of which are generally published in the same calendar year. One number is a collection of recent speeches; each of the others is devoted to a single subject and gives background information and discussion from various points of view, concluding with a comprehensive bibliography. Books in the series may be purchased individually or on subscription.

Library of Congress Cataloging in Publication Data

Reische, Diana L   comp.
    Women and society.

    (The Reference shelf, v. 43, no.6)
    Bibliography: p.
    1. Women in the United States--Addresses, essays,
lectures. 2. Women's Liberation Movement--Addresses,
essays, lectures. 3. Woman--History and condition of
women--Addresses, essays, lectures. I. Title.
II. Series.
HQ1426.R45   301.41'2'08   73-159163
ISBN 0-8242-0451-4

PREFACE

To raise the children, to stir the stew, to wash the curtains from time to time, to create a home and refuge for the rest of the family—that, with variations, has been the image of woman's ideal role. No matter that many women didn't fit the ideal, that they had to work to help support the family, or that they were divorced or single. The image itself was as secure as motherhood. But the image in whose eyes? In men's? Or in women's?

The image and the reality are far out of phase today. It isn't just the ardent Women's Liberationists who are challenging the stereotypes. Today 43 percent of all adult women in the United States work outside the home. Something is stirring, and it is not the stew. Women are restless, questioning roles their mothers played unhesitatingly.

It is difficult to tell whether this restlessness is a tidal wave of new feminism or just a rehash of the suffragette movement. But something does seem different. Perhaps it is the scope of the discontent, the breadth of the challenge to existing institutions that place women eternally in the subordinate role. A spate of books has kept the debate active: Betty Friedan's *The Feminine Mystique*, Kate Millett's *Sexual Politics*, Germaine Greer's *The Female Eunuch*—and the much earlier work of Simone de Beauvoir, *The Second Sex*.

Many factors have coalesced to stir the discontent: as women bear smaller families, their home duties are lightened. In a family with fewer children, the last child leaves home earlier, thus enabling a mother to reenter the job market earlier. More and more women have taken jobs to supplement family incomes during the expensive years of educating children. And, as more women complete college and postgraduate work, the urge to put the education to use becomes more widespread.

3

The Liberation movement has its extremists: the "hate men" judochop girls who insist that women are inherently not a bit different from men. But alongside these radicals and publicity seekers there is a hard and serious core of dissatisfied women who are pressing their claims in court, in legislatures, and on the job.

Spearheading the movement is a loosely affiliated group of generally well-educated younger women in their twenties and thirties. The traditional woman's role of tending house bores and stifles them. They are demanding options for those who reject the traditional role.

This book does not dwell long on specific leaders or organizations. They change. The issues remain.

Section I surveys the extent of the challenge to the status quo. It highlights some of the specific pressure points such as abortion law reform and women's studies.

A second section deals with the single most specific and unanimous target of women's groups: elimination of discrimination in jobs and salaries. A third section surveys the role women have played in various societies throughout history.

A final section explores the highly controversial questions of which came first: female biology or female behavior. Some feminists argue that virtually all of what is considered "feminine" behavior is the result of sexist conditioning. Current research can be marshaled to support either that position or its antithesis—inherent femininity.

No discussion of women is complete without placing them in the context of home and family. What of the children? Do they suffer if their mother goes to work? Is marriage itself an outworn institution?

There aren't many final answers available now. Nevertheless, something is afoot. Too many questions are being raised, too many women are pursuing careers, to anticipate a slide back to the old roles. The suffragettes settled for the vote. Today's activists insist that they want freedom to define for each individual woman a personally enriching role in society.

The editor wishes to thank the many authors and publishers who have generously permitted publication of their work in this volume.

DIANA REISCHE

November 1971

This paper does not intend to dwell on specific leaders or organization. They are subject to change, but the issues will remain. Therefore by investigating the legititamacy of the targets pursued by women's groups, questions concerning male oppression can be brought to light "Womens Liberation" is both a broad term

CONTENTS

III.   SOME PERSPECTIVES—SOCIAL AND HISTORICAL

IV.   BIOLOGY AND THE SOCIAL ROLE

I. THE QUEST FOR OPTIONS

EDITOR'S INTRODUCTION

The trouble with trying to pose the question "What do women want?" is that the question itself is a foolish one. It's like asking what men want. They want different, many different, and individually conflicting things.

The complaint the angry feminists of the 1970s have is that the role blithely assigned "woman" in society today is all too often a male idea of what a woman is and what should make her happy. Women are demanding equality to define individually satisfying roles without regard to some "feminine" ideal.

The quest is everywhere for options, against a single assigned place to be filled by both the gentle homebody and the restless lawyer. This section ranges over the quest for options and the areas in which that quest has generated conflict in a male-oriented society.

In the first article a writer for the Washington *Post* outlines the general goals of the Women's Liberation movement, insisting that while some women in the movement have adopted foolish tactics, the movement itself is in earnest. Next, in a lighter vein, Los Angeles *Times* women's editor Maggie Savoy expresses her annoyance with the repeated question—asked by men—of "What do they want?"

Not too surprisingly, the ranks of women aren't unanimously marching behind the feminists' self-reliant banner. *Look*'s Betty Rollin takes a not very sympathetic view of some of the organized opposition to Women's Liberation.

The next few articles survey some of the specific issues in the Women's Liberation movement to indicate the breadth of the challenge to traditional thinking about women and society. From the *Wall Street Journal* comes a survey of the

11

rising campus popularity of women's studies courses, and from *Newsweek* a look at the challenge to male dominance in the churches.

Women's groups have been insisting with increasing vehemence that women, not men, should have the right to determine whether or not they will bear children. Thus repeal of male-written abortion laws is a prime goal of Liberation groups. Richard Worsnop's article on abortion law outlines the reforms being pressed in legislatures and courts.

A concluding article is a survey conducted by *Saturday Review* of what some prominent women—and a few men—think the status of women is today in terms of the ideal and the imperfect past.

WHAT IS WOMEN'S LIBERATION REALLY ALL ABOUT? [1]

To those who have had their fill of radical movements, the reawakening of a strident women's rights movement is about as welcome as finding out that coffee causes cancer.

But reawakening it is. And the mass media have seized upon it with a vengeance. . . .

Despite the current barrage of publicity, it's difficult to find people of either sex who understand what Women's Liberation is really all about. Mainly, this is because it's one movement that has a built-in backlash before it even gets started.

For instance, David Susskind can usually be expected to listen with sympathy to any expounder of liberal causes on his TV talk show. But when it comes to Women's Liberation, he can hardly conceal his annoyance and puts it down with sarcasm and ridicule.

He's not alone. The response from almost any male—whether liberal, radical or conservative in viewpoint—ranges

[1] From "Beneath Those Charred Bras Revolution Smolders," by Mary Wiegers, staff writer. Washington *Post*. p G 1. Mr. 8. '70. Reprinted by permission.

from amusement to intense hostility. It rarely includes the openness with which they might discuss any other issue.

To many men, the issue is either one which they cannot take seriously (because they have been trained since birth about women's proper place, and any further discussion of the question is frivolous), or it is an affront to their masculinity perpetrated by a small number of uppity women.

A woman's reaction tends to be a bit different, but often no less hostile. Those who consider themselves "feminine" and have prospered by being so, feel superior and scornful of "feminists." Their attitude is: "I've made it by accommodating men and working my wiles upon them, and the fact that these women are complaining proves they are lacking in charm and feminine instincts."

And many quite honestly feel that the present position of women is the natural one. They feel secure, happy and protected in their present roles of wife and/or mother, and they resent the belittling of their position and the attempt to tear it down. Many more feel some ambivalence. They recognize and empathize with many of the points Women's Lib makes. But the movement's tactics and some of their conclusions turn them off.

Even those who support or are in Women's Liberation have an emotional problem with it. One of the most common complaints against the Women's Liberation type is that she's so "unfeminine;" that she comes on sounding strident, harsh and fanatical; that she puts people off before they even hear what she has to say.

It's a problem for women in the movement, too, causing a certain paranoia-schizophrenia. They're not sure how far they can go in asserting themselves without giving up all semblance of dignity. They're not sure how "separatist" they should be from men, or, on the other hand, how much they can associate with men without compromising their feminist principles. And, though they eschew the "myths" about what is feminine, they are sensitive to charges that they're not.

Their dilemma is partly a result of the larger question which the whole movement calls up, namely what is intrinsically female and what is intrinsically masculine. Which feminine traits are the results of biology, and which are culturally enforced?

Since it's difficult to find an unemotional response to the Women's Liberation question, it's difficult to understand what's behind it, why it's happening and what the new feminist philosophy really is.

"Women's Liberation" is both a broad term covering the whole resurgent women's rights movement and a specific term for one group within that movement.

Used in the specific sense, the term refers to the Women's Liberation movement, whose member groups are located primarily in New York, Boston, Washington, Pittsburgh, Chicago, and San Francisco. Though they generally support one another, they operate largely independently.

Used in the general sense, it refers to a gamut of organizations, from the work-within-the-system reformists like Betty Friedan's National Organization for Women (NOW) to the radical WITCH (Women's International Terrorist Conspiracy from Hell).

It's impossible to say how many belong to the movement. Anywhere from 10,000 to 50,000 activists would be a good guess.

Women's Liberation really only got started in 1968 and at this early stage is heavily reliant on hard core cells of a score or more members. It has no national organization, like the League of Women Voters, with its rolls of active members and less active supporters.

Women's Liberation is more of a philosophy than a coherent, cohesive political movement, although almost every organization has taken part in some political action, such as demonstrating against abortion laws or protesting the Miss America pageant.

Whether it will become a truly effective mass movement depends in large part on whether it reflects an idea whose time has come.

Some of the hostile reactions to "Women's Lib" are justifiable, or at least, understandable.

When Women's Liberation members first surfaced at the 1968 Miss America contest, their protest took the form of bra burning. A rash of bra burnings followed.

A Stigma of Silliness

No matter how opposed you were to sit-ins, lie-ins, marches and other demonstrations, none of them seemed to represent quite as bad a case of the sillies as bra burning. And though they had a point to make, the stigma of silliness has stuck to Women's Liberation ever since.

There are other more important points. In the beginning, the suffragettes met with scorn and ridicule, too. But, in the interest of achieving one goal—the vote—they gave up other demands, and in the end, took pains to reassure their opponents that they would remain feminine, motherly, housewifely.

. . . They believed that if they were granted their legal rights, i.e., the vote, then other rights would quickly follow, despite whatever reassurances they gave their men.

There has always been a close parallel between the civil rights movement and women's rights. The suffragette movement grew out of the abolitionist movement. And, like those who thought the Fifteenth Amendment would guarantee equality for blacks, some thought the Nineteenth Amendment would guarantee equality for women. Both were wrong, of course. And the resurgence of the women's movement once again follows the resurgence and shift in direction of the civil rights movement. Like blacks, women want, this time, not just equality under the law, but the kind of moral and social climate that can make them really free—psychologically, socially and economically.

And like blacks, they talk less now of "integration and full partnership" than of "separatism." And as blacks now question white society's values, so women are openly challenging "male-dominated" preconceptions of a proper social structure, including its basic underpinnings of marriage and the family.

These challenges are taking the form of revolt against dressing to please men; being treated as "sex objects"; being manipulated as consumers in a Madison-Avenue-motivated capitalist society; being treated as "guinea pigs" in the use of the birth control pill; not being free to decide whether to have an abortion or not; and against being treated as "chicks" by their male colleagues in the peace and campus radical movements.

In essence, the revolt is against the attitude that women are "second-class thinkers" unable to play a wholly independent role.

As suffragette Emma Guffey Miller phrased it after women were given the vote in 1917, "We're out of the idiot class, but still in the children class."

Why Did Feminism Lie Dormant So Long?

Why the women's movement lay dormant for so many years after winning the vote in 1917 is not clear. Certainly, the Depression and World War II helped to submerge it. But World War II also nurtured a sociological phenomenon which laid the basis for the present women's protest.

After World War II, there was a general retreat from the world, and a mass migration to the suburbs. This reinforced the values of family life, of feminine domesticity and motherhood.

The postwar generation of young marrieds was also a generation accustomed to sacrificing. They had sacrificed throughout the Depression and then to win the war. After the war, it was a natural next step to continue sacrificing— this time for the children. They sacrificed to buy the children material goods, education and even culture. The whole idea was expressed in the sentence, "I want my kid to have it better than I did."

It was also the age of Dr. [Benjamin] Spock who told parents that the child was a unique individual, full of potential. With careful molding and continuous attention to his rearing, they could fashion him into a well-rounded human achiever, they were told. And conversely without that attention he could be crippled for life.

Women were told that the rearing of this child was the most challenging thing they could do, which would give them a sense of fulfillment far beyond any other occupation. Men, of course, had a role in this child-rearing too, but it was recognized that the family could not be as all-consuming for them, since they still had their careers. So it was to the woman that the overriding challenge of molding the child in the Spockian manner fell. And to do this, she was to sacrifice not just a career, but a large part of her outside interests and herself.

This fostered, sociologist Philip Slater says, a "neutralized woman," without any concept of her own identity, a woman who sacrificed even her own sexuality to molding children.

Now it is this image of women that the female radicals, all young, are striking at. They cannot reassure their opponents that they'll remain feminine, motherly and housewifely. It's precisely this image of a woman as demure, deferring, acquiescent, a helpmate and mother, rather than a person in her own right, that the movement now is trying to overturn. And because they are striking at the whole structure of woman and the family in society today, people who have lived their lives taking those values for granted have some cause to be put off, angry and frightened.

Because beyond the suffragettes, ultimately Women's Liberation is questioning the traditional values of marriage and family, of capitalism, of the precept that a woman should devote most of her time to rearing children, of the idea that a married woman has a duty to spend much of her time in manual labor such as cooking and cleaning, of the notion that a single girl's main preoccupation should be getting a man—in short, the whole social and economic fabric of which the United States today is woven.

They're not the only ones questioning these things, of course, but it seems more isolated and remote, less threatening, when talked about in terms of a political movement or a sociological trend than when it's talked about in terms of mobilizing the women of the nation.

Dr. Margaret Mead has been preaching for some time now that we are on the brink of enormous change in the way society is structured. The birth of civilization, she says, freed men from servitude to the soil and opened all kinds of opportunities—in the arts, politics, science—to them. It didn't do the same for women, because women remained chained to rearing children, a necessity because of the high death rate among the young, and the need for an adequate population to carry on the work of civilization.

Now, for the first time, Dr. Mead says, there is an about-face in this situation. Because of the population explosion, women are encouraged to have less or no children. And, as this situation takes hold, she says, society must open up opportunities for women outside the family.

In fact, she argues, it must take a hard look at the family, realizing that out of loneliness and a need for protective ties, people will always band together, but considering whether marriage, or some form of tribal or communal society is better.

In Sweden communal living is spreading rapidly. In this country, the commune is still considered aberrant, but it can be found in Takoma Park as well as California.

Dr. Mead calls the new feminists "too superficial" to effect the revolutionary change she's talking about. She's probably right, but if nothing else, they may be laying the groundwork for serious consideration of the kinds of questions she's raising.

Finally, the reaction to Women's Lib does say something about the accepted attitude towards women. There is, in fact, simple prejudice at work—prejudice which says that women should be content with their lot and not stir up trouble when there are so many more "important" issues around. After all, the argument goes, women aren't starving.

Starving or not, the movement is here. It just may do away with the cliché long extolled by politicians—"God, the flag and motherhood."

"Motherhood" is no longer a safe subject.

MAN'S PRIMER TO WOMEN'S LIBERATION [2]

I'm one Woman's Libber weary of big, strong, handsome, successful, intelligent, tycoon-type males who approach me at parties (of all times!) and—instead of a healthy oblique pass—give me the puzzled hangdog question: "Maggie, what is this Woman's Lib thing all about?"

I'd show feminine compassion if they didn't invariably follow with a smirk of masculine wit, viz:

"Why incinerate lingerie?"

"What more do they want?"

"Let's draft 'em."

"They want to go to the moon in a one-biffy spaceship?"

"I promise not to think of Betty Friedan as a sex object."

"Vive la différence."

"———" (fill in your own inanity).

At this point I look around for some walleyed ex-footballer. He's no threat to me: I don't want to play his game. I'm no threat to him: He's all bone and muscle, can be hurt only with a knife. Then I melt. Poor men. They're threatened, afraid. Lysistrata might strike again. This revolution is on their home grounds. They really need reassurance.

[2] From "Man's Primer to Womlib," by Maggie Savoy, Los Angeles *Times* women's editor. Los Angeles *Times*. p E 1. N. 29, '70. Copyright, 1970, Los Angeles *Times*. Reprinted by permission.

Depending on the inquisitor I answer variously. If he's intellectual, I remind him: "Our brains weigh the same; it's our paychecks that are slim and ladylike."

If he's a politician, I simply remind him, "We outnumber you." . . .

If he says—some still do—"Woman's place is in the home," I brighten. "It's so wonderful we want to share it. Here's a dishrag."

Scratch any woman, you scratch a feminist. An angry feminist. Those who deny it the loudest or the simperiest are the real walking wounded. As one said, "I've spent fifty-two years adjusting to being a woman—I'm too tired to rock the boat." The healthy women are in there fighting.

Blunt fact: American women are second-class citizens.

They want a fair shot at the starting line.

Like other minority groups—the blacks, Chicanos, youth, consumers—they are the fighting victims of stereotyping, myths, mis- and un-truths, attitudes, prejudices, chauvinism. Like other minority groups they sometimes get hysterical, angry, prone to overstate and overreact. Overreaction, as all newspaper editors know, brings backlash, lashback, flap, flak and fury, blurs the real issues—and has been known to start wars and crusades.

I won't bore you with statistics. A third of the work force is female; 42 percent of women sixteen and older work. The median wage for which they work is 58.2 percent of men's. At the same educational level, women make about half of what men do. She needs a college degree to earn more than a man with an eighth-grade education.

Though few (some do!) consider themselves men's natural enemies, many women—to their own discomfort—become Instant Radicals at some masculine wisecrack. Their senses of humor have short fuses.

One, suing for back royalties on three hundred songs, blew her cool when the opposing lawyer looked around the courtroom and said, "Why is a mere housewife wasting these busy men's time?" She went home and wrote "Liberation Now!," the movement's official rallying song.

Another, joshing her husband to look for a woman to put on a board of directors, went bug-eyed when her husband answered, "A woman? We don't even have a black yet." . . .

Right now, lords of the universe, it is time to lift some of the guilt from your leonine heads. Women themselves are most guilty. They have raised our children. Most learned what they know today with their mother's milk (from discontented mothers). We were raised—boys and girls alike—on the separate-but-equal philosophy. Girls were to cook food, change diapers, mop floors, arrange flowers, set their hair, join a sorority, attract the most promising boy. Boys were to hunt, take math and banking, tinker with cars, join a fraternity and find that perfect little girl who, when commanded to jump, cooed, "How far?"

Times have changed. Economics have changed. The Pill is here. That is why, fifty years after men finally gave us the vote, the movement bursts open again.

Woman's role was sound economically—therefore religiously—for pioneer days. Boy babies were needed then, en masse, to hew trees, build roads, mine mines, explore frontiers, man battle lines, farm farms. Girl babies were needed then, en masse, to clean, cook, tend the fires and pump the water for Saturday night baths.

The same scientific discoveries that took men off their eighteen-hour-a-day shifts freed Mom from scut work. Her job, after the children were raised, evaporated to a few hours a day.

Last generation's woman filled in her time, exercised her brains and talents, rolling bandages, doing "good things," which more often than not required addressing envelopes, joining bridge clubs or elevating her mind with Gayelord Hauser lectures. For this she got a pat on the head from proud husband, her picture on the society page. This generation's woman—educated, trained and exposed to the same information-glut as her husband—simply is not going that route.

This generation's woman has read "The Myth of the Vaginal Orgasm," spits the word Freud like a four-letter word and refuses the double moral standard. As one said to me, "If men had to pay for their sins, abortion would be legal, free and fast."

Another cries, "Invent a Pill for men; let them bloat." Others want to share responsibility as well as the fun, shed the monthly worry most suffer thirty-five years of their lives. "After two children, vasectomy," is their cry, echoed by more and more men.

With children flown the coop, divorce or widowhood likely years ahead, she demands—will inevitably get—meaning to her life and challenge to her brain.

Four Basic Demands

Boil down all the craziness . . . their basic fourfold demands make sense:

Free, twenty-four-hour child care centers. (Daddy's split, the law can't catch him; Mommy's working at half pay. Society must take up the slack, lest it cripple still another generation.)

Free abortion, on demand. . . . (The cost of an abortion is minuscule compared with raising an unwanted child.)

Complete equality for women in employment, advancement, opportunity. With alimony on the way out, fair's fair.

Complete equality for women in education.

These are all reasonable today, require a minimum of male logic to understand.

To those who howl, "It will break down the very fabric of marriage," I point to the facts, Sir: Marriage is in one helluva state already.

To those who worry about our moral fabric: Talked to any teenagers recently?

To those who fear it will hit them where they live—smack in the middle of their comfort zones—I ask what is so comfortable about slaving in a job you probably don't want when you've got a perfectly good partner who really wants some responsibility too? I also submit Darvon/Compoz/Martini-gulping will decrease drastically; that self-realized women don't nag. . . .

What is required today of all men is mere acknowledgment that women are individuals, people.

There's not only rationality in this claim: There are good, sound, economic reasons for it. In a society based as is ours on an educated constituency and contributing workers, it's a flat-out waste of gross national product to underuse any potential talent, wherever it is.

Women ask to be judged and permitted to operate at full potential; be paid fairly for what they do; be listened to without that "dumb-blonde" look flashing in male's eyes; be given real help in the raising of children (thereby diminishing the curse of momism that pocks our society and makes homosexuals and neurotics out of too many); be treated as sexual partners.

Why should this scare you? Why should it puzzle you? If it's Future Shock that bugs you, you're going to have to cope with it anyway. You can cope far better, far more happily, with a sound, strong, potentialized partner than with a frustrated (no matter how outwardly she sweetly smiles), whimpering, sycophantic clinging vine.

To begin to understand what it's all about, you need to turn your own ears to those offhand remarks that are so hidden even most women don't hear them:

"Don't worry your pretty little head."

"Come in, Darling—we weren't talking about anything important."

"For a female . . ."

"You think like a man" (especially when paid to another woman).

"But that's good money, for a woman."

"Phi Bete from Columbia? Good. Can you take dictation?"

"That's woman's work."

"Keep 'em barefoot and pregnant; they really learn how to appreciate a man."

"Why should she go to college—she's only going to marry and have children?"

Today's woman already has her pretty little toe into the twentieth century, and she's about to jump in.

Women are different. Vive la différence. They've come a long way, Baby. But they've got a long way to go.

BACKLASH AGAINST WOMEN'S LIB [3]

The hostess, a plain woman with nice legs, poured the coffee and passed the macaroons. Her mouth, which was rarely shut, was gay. Her eyes, fastened on her husband (whose eyes were fastened on the young, pretty lady on his left), were not. Toward the end of dinner, the subject of Women's Liberation had come up. *"Really,"* said the hostess now, with a charming smile as she passed a demitasse to the object of her husband's attention, "What *do* these women want? I'm sick to death of them. Frank says [giggle] they're lesbians. I don't go *that* far, but . . ."

It's one thing to talk about equal pay," said a lady in a pants suit, "but what the hell is wrong with keeping house? Damn it, I *like* keeping house."

"It's *marvelous* therapy," said the pretty girl, who had a musical-comedy-starlet voice.

"And that Betty Friedan!" the hostess went on, "I think she is *simply* awful! Don't you think so, Frank?"

[3] From " 'They're a Bunch of Frustrated Hags,' " by Betty Rollin, reporter, National Broadcasting Company, formerly a *Look* senior editor. *Look.* 35:15-19. Mr. 9, '71. *Look Magazine* ©. Reprinted by permission.

Frank grunted as if the subject was a waste of anyone's time. . . .

Frank and his wife and the pretty girl are not about to start a countermovement against Women's Liberation. They don't think they need to, and, besides, like most Americans, they are not "movement people." Still, they are rankled by all this Women's Lib stuff they've been hearing. After all, unlike the black movement, it's not about a bunch of people they don't run into much. It's about them. Not that Frank and his wife and the pretty girl think it's about them. In fact, the way they deal with the movement is to stress adamantly that it is by and about those others—Commies, freaks, lesbians, neurotics. If extreme annoyance and name-calling indicate that something has struck too close to home, then Women's Liberation has struck in that very place.

"There's no question," says Jo-Ann Gardner, of NOW (National Organization for Women), "where the most serious opposition to the women's movement is coming from. It's men." At the extreme right of the male opposition are men like Frank, who are committed to a kind of John Wayney mansmanship and, possibly because they're not all that confident of that mansmanship, want their women clingy and frilly and/or homey and domestic. They are men whose wives, like Frank's, bore them silly, but that doesn't mean they want to lose their wives' domestic and sexual services. And it surely doesn't mean that they want to lose the power position their male/breadwinner role gives them. Meanwhile, no matter what they do, they can count on their wives not leaving them, since such women usually have nowhere to go, or feel they have nowhere to go, which adds up to the same thing. Many of these men are political conservatives. They are against change in general, and they are suspicious of people who want it. "Such men," says Dr. Gerald Gardner, Jo-Ann Gardner's husband, "are like the plantation owners who argued that life wouldn't be the same without slaves. They are right. Life won't be the same, and if you own even a small plantation, you may not like it."

Anti—Women's Liberation people tend to belong to an organized religion. They view social change as a disruption of what they believe is the natural order of things—what God intended. "If God meant women to be like men," says a Long Island farmer, "he woulda made 'em that way." He goes on to say he doesn't quite know what Women's Lib is, but "I know I don't like it." The blame-it-on-God/natural-order/biological-destiny folks aren't all farmers, however. Professor Lionel Tiger, who has become the darling of the opposition, has published article after article stressing the irrefutability of biological differences between the sexes. (Most sane Women's Libbers, by the way, don't deny biological sex differences, but they question how much difference the differences make.) Dr. Edgar Berman, a Washington physician, made waves when he suggested that a woman's menstrual cycle keeps her from being effective in high places. Many psychoanalysts, resting heavily on Freud's "anatomy is destiny" theme, find some Women's Lib tenets—particularly those having to do with vaginal orgasm—pathological.

And then there are the bland, but revealing, male remarks like: "I like women who are women," which really means: "I like women who act in a way that I learned to think—and have always thought—is the right way for women to act; women who, even if they work, are first and foremost wives and mothers; women who are feminine, agreeable and, of course, attractive to men."

Women in the movement are always saying that "When women are free [of sex-stereotyping], men will be too." But even feminists admit that, initially, anyway, men have a lot to lose. Apart from any trouble they may be having at home, men also have female employees to cope with. Not only are men being forced to give equal opportunities, but—ouch!—they're beginning to have to *pay* them equally!

This not only gets male *employers* where it hurts. It gets male *employees* too. (Remember how southern whites reacted when they feared—correctly, to be sure—that black men would compete for their jobs?) For as society's expectation of females expands to include professional activities, and as women really begin to achieve professionally, they will indeed be in competition with men. In fact, women will not be competing with their husbands or want to be, any more than their husbands want to compete in business with their brothers or fathers. But many men fear, perhaps only unconsciously, that once doors are thrown open to women, their wives will be at least represented by the women who walk in. Some professional associations and most unions are, in a stunning variety of ways, trying to protect their members from the threat of more women in the job market.

Job competition with women is also a big issue among blacks. In fact, from the Women's Lib point of view, the most embarrassing and distressing opposition has come from blacks. "How do we cope with the black male whom we can't put down and who's putting us down all over the place?" wails one feminist. Why are blacks against Women's Lib? Because, the answer goes, black males are afraid white women are after their jobs; and black females are afraid white women are after their men's jobs and, possibly, their men. Besides that, black women are not wildly empathetic with white women, whom they see as the overprivileged possessors of a lot they (black women) want. Moreover, Frances Beale, a black activist, writes, "Some young sisters who have never *had* [italics mine] to maintain a household . . . tend to romanticize (along with the help of a few brothers) this role of housewife and mother. Black women who have had to endure this kind of function are less apt to have these utopian visions."

Predictably, much female backlash is a result of male backlash. The hostess of the aforementioned dinner party is nervous enough about her husband. She isn't about to antagonize him further by going gung-ho over Women's Lib. Besides, her whole sense of her own femininity hangs on being accepting. To express positive interest in the movement would be, in itself, unfeminine. Even if they are unhappy, women, like most people, are frightened of change.

A lot of women react icily to Women's Lib because they don't want to hear, now that they think it's too late, about alternatives they might have chosen. "Some older women," says feminist Sheila Tobias, associate provost of Wesleyan University, "are just plain jealous of younger women who not only have options—to get married, have children, have careers, or *not*—but use them."

Although she may consider herself "cleverer than her husband," "foxier," "more deceitful," studies show that a woman sees herself as generally less intelligent than men. A professor of psychology at Connecticut College gave a large group of women identical articles to read. Only the by-lines differed—sometimes a woman was given as author, sometimes a man. Repeatedly, the testees rated higher the article by the "man." But what of the women who like their somebody's-wife and/or somebody's-mother identity? "I *like* being 'Neal's wife,' " says Mrs. Jane Freeman, a Mary Tyler Moorey housewife/mother. "I get great pleasure from my husband's success." Mrs. Freeman is, if there is such a thing, a perfectly adjusted American female. Although her good manners (and femininity) keep her from name-calling, it is clear that to her, Women's Lib is just a lot of noise. "Really," she says, "I saw one of those Lib women on TV. She ranted and raved so, I thought maybe she just had a bad day." Mrs. Freeman worked before she was married—at the *Reader's Digest* for $90 a week, and as manager of a senatorial campaign office, for $125. But, she says, "It never occurred to me that I wasn't being given my just reward." She is studying interior decorating because, she does admit, she was getting a bit restless being at home all the time, "but I would be unhappy if it got out of hand. . . ."

Happy housewives aren't the only anti-Libbers. Take the other ladies at the dinner party. The pretty girl eyed by the host gets a lot of mileage out of being a so-called "sex object." She is not motivated to change or alter a system that has been rewarding to her. . . . The other lady at the party ("Damn it, I *like* keeping house") turns out to be a buyer in a textile firm who does *some* of her own housework. She's been a career lady, and a successful one, all her adult life. Her attitude, similar to a black surgeon's, is, simply, I made it, why can't they? And if a woman really *wants* to, she can be successful. Some feminists call that Aunt Tomism. Others call it "the only-Jew-in-the-club" syndrome. I call it psychologically and sociologically naive. Whatever it is, it's a position often taken by women who, like male workers, just don't want a whole new batch of female competition.

Two Anti-Lib Groups: First, the Pussycats

The Pussycats are anti-Libbers who seem to be afraid Women's Lib means giving up black lace underwear. They have buttons and cute little slogans like "The lamb chop is mightier than the karate chop." But at a meeting in Miami, it turned out, surprisingly, that most of the members were career women. One, Joyce Held, a designer whose husband is also a designer, said, "I sell my own work for $100; if I say it's my husband's, I can get $1,000. But I wear feminine clothes. I wear perfume. I keep smiling." . . .

The Pussycat population runs the gamut—from name-callers to women who are for abortion and equal pay but object to what they see as the militant style of Women's Liberation. Much negative reaction to Women's Liberation is based on style or on misunderstanding of what Women's Liberation is, or on an aspect of it that is interpreted as the whole. Some enlightened people attack man-hating lesbians as if they represented the movement. Even the president of Yale has attacked "the man-hating part of the movement represented by Betty Friedan." (This writer knows for a fact that she is neither a man-hater nor the representative of a man-hating faction.) Similarly, a bra-burning, seen frequently as the symbol of Women's Lib, has more to do with fashion than liberation. Of course, some of the "misunderstanding" may be deliberate.

Jo-Ann Gardner feels, however, that among lower economic groups, ignorance about the movement is genuine.

"A lot of poor women bring complaints on sex discrimination to the NOW office—checkers at supermarkets who freeze near open doors, but are not allowed to wear pants—and they're always shocked to find that we're not freaks." For the freaky idea, Mrs. Gardner blames such "institutional backlash" as TV (except NBC) and the daily press. The other most serious institutional backlash comes from the Roman Catholic Church. Feminists interpret the Church's stand against abortion and birth control as, in effect, a stand against women. "To the Church," says Sheila Tobias, "a fetus is more important than a woman." And in the Government, a host of senators and congressmen, notably Senator Sam Ervin [Democrat, North Carolina], have reacted negatively to the pro-liberation Equal Rights Bill.

Will the backlash be effective? Women's Liberationists are no less optimistic on account of it. Says one: "Scratch a backlash lady, and you know what's underneath? A feminist."

Fascinating Womanhood

"You are indeed fascinating women," purrs Mrs. Leathen, the teacher. "You're lovely," breathes Mrs. Tubbs, the assistant. Mrs. Leathen, a fortyish, pretty lady with a Sunday-school smile, has a red bow in her hair. Mrs. Tubbs, slightly younger, has on a white-organdy ruffled blouse, ruby-red lipstick and, I think, a permanent wave. The ladies assembled —age range twenty-five to fifty—are equally ruffled, flowered, rouged and curled. On this bright morning in Fort Lauderdale, Florida, they are having their last class in Fascinating Womanhood; and they can all "hardly wait," as one of the older ladies put it, "to begin *living* the precious things we have learned." Now that the chatter has subsided and the coffee cups have been emptied, everyone has gotten comfy in the living room, and Mrs. Leathen is saying: "These principles must be learned and they must be . . ."

"Practiced," says the class in joyous unison. "And . . . ?" asks a beaming Mrs. Leathen.

"Expressed," calls out a young woman with spit curls. "If your husband ever mistreats you," Mrs. Leathen goes on, "you have learned how to be charming and fascinating in return. . . . But why isn't there a course for men?"

"They Don't Need It," comes the instant reply. Toward the end, there are testimonies. One lady tells of how she solved her difficulty in finding really feminine clothes by shopping in the children's department. Fascinating Woman-hood teaches "childlikeness," also "sauciness," as positive virtues to be employed in the improvement of any marriage.

"Childlike anger is fun," says Mrs. Leathen to another of her classes in Miami. "You'll be *glad* that your husband irritated you. It makes arguing so *charming!*"

"When I can't handle things in my marriage," says Christine Cantin, a button-cute, twenty-one-year-old wife and mother, "I say to Greg, 'Oh, I'm just a little girl,' and it works! And you know what helps? To look at your own little girl—the way she 'stamps her foot and shakes her curls' [quote from FW book], you just want to love her!"

Well, readers, you must be bursting with what killed the kat! Curiosity! Am I right? OK. (1) FW is no joke; (2) it's a rich corporation; (3) it's a book with sales, according to the author, of 200,000; (4) it's classes all over the United States with a total past and present enrollment of about 75,000; (5) it's also a fill-in-the-blanks notebook—the kind most of us haven't seen since the sixth grade. Example: "Femininity Is Achieved by Accentuating the —— Between You and Men, Not the Similarities." All of this (and more! the author's newest book is *The Fascinating Girl*) is the handiwork of fifty-year-old Helen B. Andelin of Santa Barbara, California, mother of eight and wife of ex-dentist/businessman Aubrey P., who is now president of the Andelin "Foundation." Mrs. Andelin wrote FW in '63, before the feminist movement really got going. Her philosophy and what has emerged from it is John Birchy in its opposition to Women's Liberation. The general thesis is that man must be the unconditional leader, and that the woman should strive to be an unconditional follower. She is also supposed to be a few other things, like a "domestic goddess" and "the ideal woman." From taking better care of her refrigerator to trying the dweat-big-strongman stuff on sons, the book and workbook spell out everything a woman should do with the thoroughness of a detailed sex manual—except sex.

The Andelins also put out a magazine cramful of "success stories." In reading these, one gets the impression that FW has indeed helped a lot of women change from whiny children to goody-goody children. Chris Cantin, whose family is Catholic and conservative, describes her conversion:

My mom told me about it [she says]. She told me if I went, she'd pay and buy me an outfit. So the bribe kinda helped. First, I thought the whole thing was kinda dippy. I mean I liked that it was against Women's Lib. Women's Lib is negative. I can't stand people who are negative—but I didn't want the opposite extreme either. At first, it was really hard to take—that you should always be the follower. And I used to think I should be equal in some ways—but now I don't. I still don't really understand why it's all up to the woman to make the marriage work, but I accept it. We read the Bible a lot. I'm not too religious, but God said it's women's role to be like we're taught, so I guess it is. . . . In school, I wanted to be a marine biologist." [She giggles and gives her daughter a hug.] But I got married. It used to hurt me that I wouldn't be able to use my talents, but not anymore. I still go to college. I may teach, but that's OK. It's a woman's role. Greg doesn't really like me going to school. I think he's a little bit afraid that I'll catch up with him. If it's going to bother him if I continue my education, then I won't, I mean, who am I? I mean it's very important to me, but not that important, know what I mean?

WOMEN'S STUDIES ON THE CAMPUSES [4]

"In the beginning, women were usually pregnant, so the men hunted and fished while the women stayed home."

So begins the tale of women's oppression as told by Cranky Productions, a theatre group appearing on and around the San Diego State College campus. . . . Accom-

[4] From "Boosting 'Liberation': Women's Studies Rise in College Popularity," by Barbara Isenberg, staff reporter. *Wall Street Journal.* p 1. Je. 9, '71. Reprinted by permission.

panied by the sounds of drums, tambourine and oboe, the narrator uses drawings to trace the second-class status of women from caveman days to modern times. One drawing shows a sad-faced woman with the word "inferior" stamped on her forehead.

To improve the self-image of women and alleviate injustices, the production suggests that the women in the audience enroll in the college's year-old women's studies program, which sponsors Cranky. Courses in the program discuss such subjects as the role of women in history and literature and how society allegedly encourages feminine docility. The object is to help women understand their "oppression," so that they can do something about it.

Like black studies courses a few years ago, women's studies programs now are proliferating. American colleges and universities currently offer at least two hundred courses in women's studies, up from only seventeen in September [1970], estimates Know, Inc., a Pittsburgh publisher of feminist literature. An estimated one hundred colleges now offer such courses, and this summer many additional institutions will be preparing similar offerings.

At some campuses, the courses are having a drastic impact and creating a lively controversy. Many courses encourage militant feminism, and the programs have even prompted a few students to divorce their husbands.

In a variety of ways, the courses help students understand the status of women. At the start of a Cornell University women's history course, students were asked to list twelve famous American women who lived before 1900. "Nobody could do it," says senior Deborah Spitz, a teaching assistant in the course. "Now I expect all of them could."

At San Diego State, a course in human sexuality attempts to improve women's concept of themselves. A recent meeting of the course started with a seemingly innocuous film called "Why Man Creates." This depicted men working diligently in laboratories, doing research and studying. Women were shown as mothers, helpers to the men and ornaments. "This

is what I call an obscene film," Professor Lois Kessler told
the class. Contending the film conveyed a "sexist" view of
men creating while women merely watched, she asked the
class, "What kind of image does woman have of herself after
seeing films like this her whole life?"

The most commonly taught courses deal with women in
literature, as either authors or characters. At Mount Holyoke
College in Massachusetts, Professor James Ellis says he offered
a course last year called "Daughters and Ducats," which he
said examined "the near-chattel status of women in match-
making arrangements and the vicious double standard accompanying this most prominently in Restoration Comedy."
(A ducat is a gold coin.)

Some courses are changing lives. At Douglass College,
the women's branch of New Jersey's Rutgers University,
Professor Elaine Showalter says students have actually gotten
divorced after taking her women's studies course. "Although
their husbands threaten me, I can't feel it was my fault,"
she says. The coursework led to "a process of sensitizing
women to the political and cultural aspects of their lives. . . .
They now find that motivation can work in fields besides
housework," she says.

At the same college, a girl was planning to take a job
and pay her fiancé's way through medical school. After
taking a women's studies course, she decided she wanted
to attend medical school, too. Result: she and her fiancé
agreed they would both attend. The boy will go first—but
only because he's older, the girl insists.

At the University of Washington, women's studies led
one instructor to revert to use of her maiden name and later
to divorce her husband. She has since turned her home into
a halfway house where women in the midst of divorce
proceedings live together and adjust to their changed way
of life.

The courses often lead to political activity too. At San Diego State, students in the program sell feminist literature, give speeches to the community and support legislators working on profeminist bills. They recently picketed a bridal product exhibition that they contend treated women as a consumer but not as a person. "Why does he make the decision and she make dinner?" one picket sign asked.

Picketing and other outside activities aren't part of the regular course work. Such activities are voluntary, but they are encouraged in class, and many women do choose to volunteer. Students praise the activism of the programs. The women's studies program "is an instrument of the larger feminist movement," says San Diego State junior Pam Cole. "Ultimately it's an organizing tool, getting a woman to realize her own oppression so she can deal with it."

The activist aspects of the new courses worry some faculty members, however. Some feel the courses mainly reiterate Women's Liberation clichés. Women activists in such programs "all talk as if they ordered their words from Sears Roebuck," complains James Julian, a journalism professor at the college.

But such reservations aren't stopping women's studies. In fact, the courses are even appealing to men. Of the five hundred Cornell students enrolled in women's studies courses this year, one hundred were male. At San Diego State, men can't vote at the program's meetings, but still constitute 10 percent of the enrollment. Bill Ritter, a student in the college's women in history course, feels such study "will eliminate any male chauvinism I have left in me."

Even in some high schools, women's studies are on the way. Sydney Spiegel, social studies teacher at East High School in Cheyenne, Wyoming, says he will teach an elective course next year on the history of women. Mr. Spiegel, who taught a black history course, earlier, says the course is already attracting a great deal of attention.

WOMEN IN THE CHURCHES [5]

> But I permit not a woman to teach, nor to usurp authority over the man, but to be in silence. For Adam was first formed, then Eve. And Adam was not deceived, but the woman, being deceived, was in the transgression.
>
> —St. Paul's First Epistle to Timothy 2:11-14

Pity poor Eve. Not only was she plucked like some spare part from the chest of Adam just to keep him company, but she was later accused by St. Paul of causing the fall of man, as if original sin were a disease like hemophilia—which affects males but is transmitted only by females. Among today's liberated women, of course, St. Paul rates a high place on the list of all-time male chauvinists—and for good reason. Invariably, his strictures are cited by those who oppose granting women equal authority with men in the running of their churches. For example, Pope Paul VI recently broke with tradition to name two female saints doctors of the church, but he took pains to recall St. Paul's "severe words" against ordaining women. "Even today," he declared " a woman is not destined to have ministerial and magisterial functions in the hierarchy."

But the role of women within the Roman Catholic Church may no longer be up to the Pope alone. At the semiannual meeting of the US Catholic hierarchy next month [December 1970], a coalition of women's organizations plans to confront the assembled bishops with a series of unprecedented demands. Among the most radical:

> The opening up of "all liturgical functions" to women. "This means the diaconate, the priesthood—everything," explains Dr. Elizabeth Farians, a theologian who directs the new Joint Committee of Organizations Concerned About the Status of Women in the Catholic Church.

[5] From "Faith of Our Feminists; Question of Ordination. *Newsweek.* 76:81 N. 2, '70. Copyright Newsweek, Inc., November 2, 1970. Reprinted with permission.

An "unequivocal statement" from the bishops de-
nouncing the immorality of antifeminism in society and
in the church

The opening of all seminaries and church-related
schools to women

Introduction of mandatory "women study courses"
for all men preparing for the priesthood to help them
overcome what Farians calls the celibate clergyman's
"bachelor psychosis"

The ordination of women seems to be a problem only
among those religions that invest the priesthood with pro-
found sacramental significance. Of some twenty-five US denominations that now permit female ordination, nearly half
are of the fundamentalist variety that draws few distinctions
between clergy and laity. On the other hand, the Roman
Catholic Church, with its emphasis on the special character
of the priesthood, refuses to ordain women—as do the Orthodox churches.

Other denominations with male-only clergies seem to be
moving toward heterosexual hierarchies—but hesitantly.
Earlier this month, the General Convention of the Episcopal
Church ended a quarter century of debate by admitting
women as voting delegates to its House of Deputies. In a
companion move, however, clerics in the House of Deputies
succeeded in quashing a movement to admit women to orders
as well. The rebuff was not unexpected. "You find in scaling
the church ladder," observes Dr. Leonard Swidler, a Catholic
theologian at Temple University, "that as the ministry is
given more power and status, there is greater reluctance to
allow women a piece of it."

Indeed, even among the liberal Protestants who attach
less importance to the priesthood, ordained women find it
difficult to achieve parity with male ministers. "The real
opponents of a female clergy," says the Reverend Tilda
Norberg, who ministers to a congregation in Staten Island,
New York, with her husband, "are male ministers who feel

threatened if they have to treat women as colleagues. They can only relate to us if we do secretarial chores, pour coffee and, above all, work largely with the children."

Salary: Of the estimated seven thousand women ministers in the United States, most *do* work with children, or else in some other post under male direction. And when a woman pastor succeeds in building up a run-down church, she rarely receives a call to a wealthier, more prestigious parish. "Poor congregations recognize this," says the Reverend Elsie Gibson, author of a recent study entitled "When the Minister Is a Woman." "They know they can get a good woman to work for a salary that even mediocre male ministers might not accept."

Not surprisingly, more and more women ministers are now banding together to demand equal rights in church. To "raise the consciousness" of their colleagues, women in the United Methodist Church cite various statistical studies to prove, as church official Peggy Billings puts it, "that discrimination against women in the organized church is worse than it ever was." Miss Billings, who heads the women's division of the church's Board of Missions, charges that "women are shut out of decision making on almost all levels, get paid less than men and are not in the top executive posts."

Strings: One obvious way for women to fight such discrimination is through the pocketbook. . . . [In 1969] Methodist women raised $10 million for the church's home and foreign missions—with no bargaining strings attached. "We intend to change that this year," warns one Methodist feminist. "What male organization would allocate $10 million annually and ask for nothing in return, not even a fair shake?"

Many militant churchwomen see the ultimate goal of their movement as a liberation for all factions in the church. Catholic feminists, for example, support priests' demands for a married clergy, even though they fear that too many women might remain content with the role of the wife of a monsignor on the rise. The traditionally deferential attitude of some Catholic nuns, on the other hand, seems to pose a special problem. In the diocese of Dubuque, Iowa, which permits nuns to distribute Communion to members of their own convents, many of the older nuns refuse to accept the consecrated host from female hands.

Victim: Even so, basically conservative organizations like the National Council of Catholic Women are beginning to exhibit a new self-consciousness about their status. At the NCCW's annual convention . . . [November 1970], officials urged delegates to demand their rights—already established in principle by Vatican Council II—to offer certain prayers from the pulpit, distribute Communion and participate in dialogue sermons. "We have never been part of the feminist movement, and never hope to be," says retiring president Mrs. Norman Folda. "But the NCCW is committed to helping women achieve their full measure of justice."

For more radical churchwomen, however, justice seems to require a reexamination of Scriptural sources in the light of modern notions about sexual equality. Even doughty St. Paul, they contend, was simply a victim of the misogynistic attitude of the prevailing Jewish culture. Such cultural biases, of course, continue in the church today—even among prelates who recognize the justice of the feminist cause. "I can't see any theological reason against women in the priesthood," says Bishop Christopher Butler, a Catholic theologian. "But I hope I'm not alive when it happens."

ABORTION LAW REFORM [6]

Reform of restrictive state laws on abortion gives every indication of being an idea whose time has come. The author of a standard work on the subject could say four years ago that "abortion is the dread secret of our society." Secretiveness has since given way with astonishing speed to open discussion, legislative action, and litigation. Starting with Colorado in 1967, no fewer than fifteen states have revised

[6] From report by Richard L. Worsnop, a staff writer. *Editorial Research Reports*. 2, no 4:545-54. Jl. 24, '70. Reprinted by permission.

their penal codes with a view to broadening the legal grounds for operations to terminate pregnancy. . . .

Abortion stirs deep emotions among religious leaders, physicians, and laymen. Many persons feel that terminating the existence of a fetus, no matter how small and undeveloped it might be, is a highly repugnant act. On the other hand, an apparently growing number of persons accepts the view that abortion is needed, along with contraception, to control population growth. Militant women's groups argue, in addition, that laws governing abortion deny women full control over their own bodies.

Opinion on abortion reform is fairly evenly split. A Gallup Poll posed the following question in November 1969: "Would you favor or oppose a law which would permit a woman to go to a doctor to end pregnancy at any time during the first three months?" Of those responding, 40 percent were in favor of such a law, 50 percent were opposed, and 10 percent had no opinion. Louis Harris obtained very similar results in a poll published June 22, 1970. His polling organization sounded out opinion on laws "permitting abortion for almost any reason." Breaking down the results in terms of the respondents' religious affiliation, Gallup reported 31 percent and Harris 30 percent of Catholics in favor of more liberal abortion laws. Harris also asked for opinions on the statement that "Until good, safe birth-control methods can be found, abortions should be legalized." Forty-nine percent of the respondents agreed with the statement, and 39 percent disagreed.

Recent Enactment of Lenient Abortion Statutes

Of the fifteen most recent abortion laws, twelve [those of Arkansas, California, Colorado, Delaware, Georgia, Kansas, Maryland, New Mexico, North Carolina, Oregon, South Carolina, and Virginia] are derived from the American Law Institute's proposed Model Penal Code provisions on the subject. Section 230.3 of the code would legalize abortion (1) to preserve the physical or mental health of the mother;

or (2) if the pregnancy has resulted from rape or incest; or (3) when doctors agree that there is a substantial risk that the child will be born with a grave physical or mental defect. All twelve states permit abortions under the first and second conditions, and nine of the states permit abortions under the third condition. Other provisions of abortion laws, whether new or old, differ from state to state. Residence requirements, when specified, vary from thirty days to four months, and the time limit during which an abortion may legally be performed, as based on length of pregnancy, ranges from sixteen to twenty-six weeks. Moreover, there is variation in requirements for medical approval of abortion. . . .

The dozen reform laws based on the model code were passed in the expectation that legal abortions would become easier to obtain and that fewer women would have to resort to dangerous illegal operations. However, the reform laws have raised almost as many problems and ambiguities as they eliminated. Reform has meant little to poor women, who cannot afford the hospital and surgical fees for legal abortions, to say nothing of the fees for psychiatric consultations required by some states. As a result, thousands of illegal abortions still are performed in states with reform laws. Another complicating factor is the reluctance of some physicians and some hospitals to handle abortions, either on moral grounds or because of uncertainty about their liabilities under the new laws. Some supporters of abortion reform have become disillusioned. State Representative Richard Lamm [Democrat] chief sponsor of reform legislation in Colorado, said the law "just isn't good enough." He added: "We tried to change a cruel, outmoded, inhuman law—and what we got was a cruel, outmoded, inhuman law."

A different approach to abortion law reform, one amounting virtually to repeal, has been taken in three states that approved new legislation on the subject in 1970—Alaska, Hawaii, and New York. In Alaska and Hawaii, abortions for any reason now are legal if performed in a hospital by a licensed physician on a "nonviable fetus"—that is, one which cannot survive outside the womb. In general, a fetus does not become viable until after the sixth month of pregnancy. Alaska has a residence requirement of thirty days and Hawaii of ninety. The New York law is essentially the same as the other two, except that there is no residence requirement and no requirement that abortions be performed in a hospital. They can, in other words, be performed in clinics or even, if circumstances permit, a doctor's office.

Since New York's abortion law now is the most liberal in the nation, hospitals and physicians in the state have been deluged with inquiries from women wishing to terminate unwanted pregnancies. A New York *Times* survey of 42 hospitals in New York City and upstate indicated that 147 abortions were performed on July 1 [1970], the date the new law took effect. Additional abortions were reported to have taken place in doctors' offices. The municipal hospital system of New York City is prepared to perform up to 25,000 or 30,000 abortions a year on city residents.

A heated debate has arisen in New York City over an attempt by the Board of Health to amend the city health code so that all legal abortions would be confined to hospitals or well-equipped clinics. Leaders of the abortion-repeal movement argue that the amendment would cancel, in New York City, intended benefits of the new state law. Unless a physician is permitted to perform an abortion in his office, they maintain, the operation becomes too expensive for low-income and middle-income women. While the Board of Health pondered and listened to the foregoing arguments on July 15, it was being picketed outside by about seventy-five young women from an abortion referral agency called Women's Abortion Project.

Court Challenges to Restrictions, Old and New

Restrictions on abortion are being attacked even more severely in court than in state legislatures. The plaintiffs in such cases contend that reform laws enacted to date are only little better than those they replaced, for the state still retains the power to define the conditions under which an abortion may be performed. The California Supreme Court, in a decision handed down on September 5, 1969 (*People v. Belous*), in effect supported this argument. The court struck down the state's 1850 abortion law, which forbade such operations "unless . . . necessary to preserve [the woman's] life." It was declared to be unconstitutionally vague and a violation of the due process clause of the Fourteenth Amendment of the United States Constitution. The 1850 statute had already been replaced by a reform law enacted in 1967; all the same, the California Supreme Court seemed to cast doubt on the constitutionality of all remaining unreformed state abortion laws.

The constitutional rights affirmed by the court in the Belous case were "the woman's rights to life [because childbirth involves risks of death] and to choose whether to bear children." Citing the United States Supreme Court opinion in *Griswold v. Connecticut,* which struck down that state's birth-control law, the California court stated: "The fundamental right of the woman to choose whether to bear children follows from the Supreme Court's and this court's repeated acknowledgment of a 'right of privacy' or 'liberty' in matters related to marriage, family, and sex." In the view of the California court, "The critical issue is not whether such rights exist, but whether the state has a compelling interest in the regulation of a subject which is within the police powers of the state." The court noted that abortions, as well as all other kinds of surgery, are less hazardous today than in 1850. "It is now safer for a woman to have a hospital therapeutic abortion during the first trimester [three months] than to bear a child."

Moreover, the California statute was held in violation of the Fourteenth Amendment because of the "delegation of decision-making power to a directly involved individual."

As the court interpreted it, the statute delegated to the doctor "the duty to determine whether a pregnant woman has the right to an abortion." The court further noted that the physician "is subject to prosecution for a felony and to deprivation of his right to practice medicine if his decision is wrong."—"Rather than being impartial, the physician has a 'direct, personal, substantial, pecuniary interest in reaching a conclusion' that the woman should not have an abortion." The state "has skewed the penalties in one direction: *no* criminal penalties are imposed where the doctor refuses to perform a necessary operation, even if the woman should in fact die because the operation was not performed."

Slightly more than two months after the California Supreme Court rendered its decision in the Belous case, Judge Gerhard A. Gesell of the United States District Court for the District of Columbia declared unconstitutional that part of the D.C. statute outlawing abortions other than those done "for the preservation of the mother's life or health." Commenting on the vagueness of this phrase, Gesell took note of the argument that the words "improperly limit the physician in carrying out his professional responsibilities." The judge's own response to the argument was that the physician "is placed in a particularly unconscionable position under the conflicting and inadequate interpretations of the D.C. abortion law now prevailing."

In a third case, a three-judge Federal panel at Dallas overturned the 111-year-old Texas abortion law, June 19, 1970, on the ground that it violated rights guaranteed by Amendments Nine through Fourteen of the United States Constitution. "Freedom to choose in the matter of abortions has been accorded the status of a 'fundamental right,'" the panel held. The United States Supreme Court has agreed to review the Gesell decision affecting the District of Columbia abortion law; its opinion in the case is bound to be a landmark, one way or another, in the fight for abortion law reform.

Reasons for Abortions: Legal Versus the Popular

A glaring defect of most state abortion laws, including
the twelve relatively new ones based on recommendations of
the American Law Institute, is that they take no account of
the primary reason why abortions are sought. Relatively few
women who want abortions have been exposed to German
measles or to drugs that might cause a deformed fetus; few
have serious heart or liver conditions that would constitute
a threat to life if they carried the pregnancy to term; and
fewer still have been the victims of rape or incest. A woman
writer [Alice S. Rossi, a professor of sociology] contended:

It is the situation *of not wanting a child* that covers the main rather
than the exceptional abortion situation. But this fact is seldom
faced. . . . Many people are unwilling to confront this fact because
it goes counter to the expectation that women are nurturant, loving
creatures who welcome every new possibility of adding a member
of the human race.

A survey conducted by the National Opinion Research
Center in December 1965 showed that of the 1,484 respondents, 71 percent approved of a legal abortion if the woman's
own health were seriously endangered by pregnancy; 56 percent if the woman had become pregnant as a result of rape;
and 55 percent if there were a strong chance that the baby
would be born with a serious defect. On the other hand, the
survey showed that only 21 percent of the respondents
favored a legal abortion if the reason was that the woman
had a low income and could not afford any more children;
18 percent if she was not married and did not want to marry
the father of her child; and 15 percent if she was married
and wanted no more children.

Medical progress reduces the need of abortions for the
very reasons which have the widest support—those of health
of the mother and child. As tuberculosis has declined as a
major health problem, for example, so has it declined as a
justification for a legal abortion. Persons who oppose repeal
of abortion laws are sometimes accused of believing, consciously or unconsciously, that the risky and degrading ex-

perience of obtaining an illegal abortion is a just punishment for the woman who is poor or unmarried or already has a large family. In other words, "If you play, you must pay."

An abortion can be a simple or a complicated medical procedure, depending on a multitude of factors. Generally speaking, though, the earlier pregnancy is terminated the safer the procedure. Four medically accepted abortion procedures are used in the United States. . . . Ideally, an abortion should be performed on a woman pregnant ten weeks or less who already has given birth to one or more children. In women who never have had a child, the cervix opening is only about the diameter of a broom straw. Thus, the dilation procedure can be time-consuming and difficult, and it often requires general anesthesia.

Issues of Population Control and Women's Rights

Abortion always has been a controversial issue in its own right. But lately it has been adopted as an ancillary cause by advocates of women's rights and of population control. This broadening of support no doubt accounts in large part for the series of successes won in recent years by proponents of abortion law reform. All abortions are of course performed on women, yet existing laws on the subject have been devised almost exclusively by men.

As recently as September 1967, women accounted for fewer than 10 percent of the delegates to the International Conference on Abortion held in Washington, D.C. By way of contrast, when the New York Joint Legislative Committee on Public Health considered abortion reform legislation on February 13, 1969, a group of angry women broke up its meeting with their demands for repeal instead of reform. "All right, now," one of the group shouted, "let's hear from some real experts—the women!" Militant feminists contend that present abortion laws constitute "cruel and unusual punishment" or "an unlawful invasion of privacy"—or even "man's vengeance on woman."

Abortion reform is one of many concerns of such groups as Zero Population Growth, whose overall aim is what its name suggests—to halt population growth. . . .

One of the strongest arguments advanced by supporters of abortion reform in the United States is that present laws discriminate against poor women. Middle-class and wealthy women can have safe abortions performed abroad. Numbers of American women have gone to Britain for legal abortions since that country liberalized its abortion laws in 1968. It has been estimated that of the 35,000 legal abortions taking place yearly in Britain, about 5,000 are performed on American women. It will be recalled that in a widely publicized case in 1962, a television personality in Phoenix, Sherri Finkbine, went to Sweden to obtain a legal abortion upon being refused the operation in Arizona.

The poor cannot afford to travel, and even under most of the recent reform laws they must pay for the time of the physicians who sign their letters, attend consultations, and sit on review panels. The woman usually must pay not only for the surgeon's services but also for administrative permission for the services. Psychiatric and surgical fees alone tend to place the cost of a legal abortion out of reach of poor women. Even in New York State, where consultation and psychiatric fees no longer are necessary, the cost of an abortion can be substantial. Although indigents are entitled to free abortions at city hospitals in New York, low-income persons who are not on welfare must pay the going rate.

Two private hospitals in New York City—Park East and Park West—have set a charge of $575 for a minimum stay of twenty-four hours. That sum includes the cost of physicians' services and laboratory tests, and there is no additional cost if the patient has to stay more than one day. Various voluntary, nonprofit hospitals in the city have reported plans for establishing single-day charges ranging from $100 to $300, with physicians' fees added in some cases. In states with abortion laws less liberal than New York's, the cost of a legal operation performed in a hospital may run as high as $600 to $700.

It may be that the only way to make abortion equally available to all would be to charge for such operations on the basis of ability to pay. Poverty-stricken women might pay nothing to have a pregnancy terminated, while well-to-do women might pay more than the actual cost. Unless some such flexible system is established, illegal abortionists probably will continue to flourish. Various experts estimate that as many as one million illegal abortions are performed in the United States each year.

WOMEN'S STATUS FIFTY YEARS AFTER THE VOTE [7]

[In 1969] Angie Elizabeth Brooks was elected President of the twenty-fourth General Assembly of the United Nations. Ironically, although both Miss Brooks of Liberia and Mrs. Vijaya Lakshmi Pandit of India, who held the same office in 1953, come from so-called "less developed" countries, they have achieved a distinction beyond the realistic aspiration today of any American woman. Is the majority sex in the United States still subjected to minority treatment? And, if so, why, *Saturday Review* asked a sampling of women—and men—concerned with male-female equality.

To begin with, how, we inquired, would you evaluate women's current status in American society—fifty years after the adoption of the Nineteenth Amendment? "As having made considerable progress, but having yet some way to go," replied the author of *The Natural Superiority of Women*, anthropologist Ashley Montagu. "Unquestionably higher than ever," said Maurine B. Neuberger, former United States Senator [Democrat] from Oregon. "Better, but overrated and hypocritical," stated the rising young journalistic star Gloria Steinem. "Revolutionary progress toward equal-

[7] From "What Did the Nineteenth Amendment Amend?" by Rochelle Girson, book review editor. *Saturday Review.* 52:29. O. 11, '69. Copyright 1969 Saturday Review, Inc. Reprinted by permission.

ity," said Eliot Janeway, who wrote *The Economics of Crisis,* "has been complicated by more than equal burdens of family responsibility, but fortified by increasing residues of capital accumulation." Bess Myerson, . . . Commissioner of the Department of Consumer Affairs of the City of New York, agreed that women's status is "considerably improved." "Liberation," observed the former Miss America and TV luminary, "has been due in great measure to technological advances." Not so, countered . . . [Dr.] Alice S. Rossi . . . [professor of sociology]. She discerns but "minimal improvement, and only so far as it is useful to the manpower needs of the society to 'permit' women to move into high-need fields. The general pressure on women," she said, "remains the same—to be the 'shock absorbers' of the society. Politically and in professions there is as low and in some fields a smaller proportion of women than twenty-five years ago." Elizabeth Fisher, founder of *Aphra,* a new publication for women, concurred. "There are barely token women in the highest spheres of politics, business, and intellectual circles." "Women's situation has been upgraded," said Long Island's most famous housewife, Billie Paget, who is by-lined "Penelope Ashe" on the novel *Naked Came the Stranger.* "But the battle of the sexes continues. Man has created woman out of his own image of what she should be. Why then is he so disappointed in his handiwork?"

"Do you feel that women still suffer discrimination in business, politics, and the professions?" we asked. "Yes, yes, and again yes!" said Miss Steinem. "This is most notable in politics," said Mrs. Neuberger. Mr. Janeway thought not. Though he finds decreasing discrimination against women in the professions, there is "less in politics than anywhere else. Much too much," he suggested, "is due to cultural lag in corporate management." The situation, remarked . . . [Miss Myerson], is "in a way comparable to the status of minorities whose individuals have to perform exceptionally to prove themselves—as it were, climbing up to a plateau from which men (or members of a majority) start a *priori.*"

"I do not *feel* women suffer discrimination," said Mrs. Rossi, "I *know* they do. My research files and personal correspondence are chock-full of such instances."

Who or what is to blame? "There has been a backlash," said Miss Fisher. "A beleaguered male population, desperately hanging onto a manhood threatened by automation, advertising, the general passivity of industrialized culture, shores up its failing strength by turning on those even lower on the scale." "Yes," said Mrs. Paget, "the men who previously had these 'preserves' all to themselves feel creatively castrated by having the 'weaker sex' compete with them." Miss Steinem holds that "a false view of what is masculine and what is feminine" is responsible; Dr. Montagu, "the bigotry of men"; . . . [Miss Myerson], "the sociological lag of the USA compared to some other cultures." In management, said Mr. Janeway, "committee-itis" is the culprit. "In higher education, the genteel tradition, fortified by male trade unionism." Women themselves are partly at fault, conceded Mrs. Neuberger. "Education and the curriculum are more to blame. Girls are not counseled to enter some of the areas which are thought of as men's arena."

Commenting on the disdain that college men today have for ambition, "which is equated with greed or with personal rivalry and striving for mere status," David Riesman, the author of *The Lonely Crowd,* said in his recent Convocation Address at Chatham College in Pittsburgh,

The consequences for college women of the altered attitudes of college men are hard to assess. Men who are themselves less competitive may feel less threatened by active career-minded women, and they may no longer care to monopolize certain kinds of prestigeful positions. However, since men still set the cultural pace and style, the current tendency to reject careers and ambition catches women at that point in their development as an oppressed group when they have not yet quite made it in terms of careers and ambition. They are a little in the position of the upwardly mobile person who is suddenly told, in a good college which he has striven to reach, that ambition is simply a hang-up, that striving is a sign of inauthenticity, and that it is more important to *be* than to *do*.

"It is far easier," said Mrs. Rossi,

to change laws which presently penalize women as workers, students, or citizens than it will be to effect social changes in family life and higher education, which depress the aspirations and motivations of women. We have yet to devise a means to compensate for the influence of parents who depress a daughter's aspiration to become a physician while urging a son to aspire beyond his capacity or preference.

Nearly all the respondents agreed that in occupations other than those dependent on physical strength women have proved themselves worthy of equality with men insofar as salary and position are concerned. "Even more so!" declared Dr. Montagu. "They've civilized most positions into which they have entered." The question annoyed Mrs. Rossi.

I find objectionable any query [she said] that asks if women have "proved themselves worthy"—by what standard? Why should they be expected to be the same in commitment or productivity when society does all it can to depress their aspirations, makes it only possible to have a significant family life plus career at enormous physical and psychological cost, lets them in only if they are really "exceptional"? The problem still is seen as why are women less productive than men, and how to make it possible for women to be as productive as men. The question should be "Why are men so driven? How can life be made more reasonable for them?" It is not even clear that women's performance is *not* "up to men's."

Bess Myerson saw no need for, nor does she take seriously, a revival of the feminist movement. Eliot Janeway dismisses it, too. But to Miss Fisher one of the most hopeful developments of our time is "the almost spontaneous growth of the Women's Liberation movement, preceded by the more conservative National Organization of Women. Women's Liberation," she said, "realized something that NOW members did not, at least initially: To ask for a bigger piece of the pie won't work. You must change the pie, throw out the patriarchal family system, which today exists in fractured form anyway, find a new family system that allows autonomy and equality for man and woman—a formidably difficult task no doubt, but an absolutely essential one, given the present decadent state of the family."

Gloria Steinem takes the current feminist movement seriously indeed.

I believe [she said] it will surpass the civil rights movement—fundamentally—in bringing societal change. The Women's Liberation movement cuts across all groups. Black and white women have already made coalitions with each other because of it. SDS [Students for a Democratic Society] girls have made coalitions with lower-middle-class suburban women. Engels said the nineteenth century paternalistic family system was the model for capitalism—that the father owned the wife, the means of production, and the children were the labor, and that society would never change until the family system changed. It has changed somewhat, has regrouped according to age and occupation (old with old, young with young, etc.) more than according to family, but we don't want to admit it, and this makes for hypocrisy and tension. Woman's Liberation is also man's liberation: from alimony, from childlike boring women, from unfair responsibility for another adult's life. When women really take a responsibility for their own lives it will be a very revolutionary change and a very good one.

Because the new development is "not a renascence of the same old 'feminism'—confined to 'vote' or to 'work,' " Mrs. Rossi pointed out, " 'revival' is the wrong word. What is new is the shift to 'liberation' of women, critically concerned with not just politics and occupation but all segments of life: household, child care, fertility, politics, art, work, leisure, etc. This is the new note." However, she warned,

since women typically live in greater intimacy with men than they do with other women, there is a potential conflict within family units when women press hard for sex equality. Their demands are on predominantly male legislators and employers in the public domain, husbands and fathers in the private sector. A married black woman can affiliate with an activist civil rights group with no implicit threat to her marriage; for a married woman to affiliate with an activist woman's rights group may very well trigger tension in her marriage. This places a major brake on the development of sex solidarity among women.

David Riesman noted that

women are not able even in a women's college to create the solidarity that is at least adumbrated or hoped for among other dis-
advantaged groups such as blacks. This is understandable, ... since
women are tied as daughters, sisters, girlfriends, or spouses to men,
whether they like it or not; they cannot create an autonomous sub-
culture of women. Women must live in the enemy camp, perhaps
one reason why the tone of the Women's Liberation movement at
times has become so shrill.

Perhaps, as Mrs. Rossi concludes, "until women learn to
achieve solidarity as a sex and fight this out politically, they
will continue to be grateful for 'crumbs' instead of fighting
for what is their due."

II. WOMEN IN THE MARKETPLACE

EDITOR'S INTRODUCTION

Never does the myth of the little woman ensconced happily at home with the children while the man labors out in the world seem farther from reality than when one glances at our labor force statistics. As of 1970, 43 percent of all adult women were out of the house earning a paycheck.

While motherhood does keep many women at home, there are nevertheless millions of other mothers holding jobs —even mothers with young children. A surprising 29 percent of mothers with children under six years of age are employed.

Almost universally, however, women are paid less and promoted less often than men in the same jobs. Discrimination in the marketplace is a major target of the Women's Liberation movement, and one that attracts and unifies many women who reject other Liberation goals.

The first article in this section gives a statistical profile of the female labor force from a management point of view. The article notes, too, that economic need is not always the reason women work. The second article details trends in the educational attainment of women, while the third selection shows the direct correlation between the level of education reached by a woman and the likelihood that she will work. Fifty-five percent of all female college graduates are employed, while 70 percent of those with graduate degrees work. Since these women are likely to be married to high-income professionals, it is clear that economic motives are not the only ones at work.

Next, Jerry Flint of the New York *Times* surveys the many instances of employment bias and work rules that discriminate against working women. He finds that challenges against these rules and discriminatory practices are increasingly successful. The most specific of these challenges are in the courts, and in the succeeding article Eileen Shanahan brings up to date the many legal challenges to sex discrimination in employment.

The final article in this section, an excerpt from an *Editorial Research Reports* analysis of the status of women, puts the conflict over jobs in the context of the overall feminist movement.

Several of the authors in this section note that women themselves—by their withdrawal from the job market, by their unwillingness to transfer on the job—are often responsible for the disparities in salaries and promotions. Thus the discussion moves on to the next two sections which put women in a historical and then a cultural context.

WOMEN IN THE LABOR FORCE [1]

This year over thirty million, or about two out of every five adult American women, will be earning a paycheck and three out of every four of them will be working on a full-time basis. Since the end of World War II, the size of the female labor force has grown more than twice as fast as the nation's total employed population.

There are many explanations for the rise in the number of women who apparently prefer the labor force to the kitchen. Financial need is certainly an important one. But it should also be observed that the increase has been experienced in a period of extraordinary prosperity. More than economic need, evidently, is at work here.

Another important factor is an ongoing escalation in the educational accomplishments of women. Over the past ten years, for example, the number achieving a high school diploma increased by 50 percent, and those attending college, by over 70 percent. Accompanying this development have been the changing needs of government and business, spe-

[1] Article by Fabian Linden of the National Industrial Conference Board Department of Consumer Economics. *Conference Board Record.* 7:37-9. Ap. '70. Reprinted by permission.

cifically the expansion in office and white-collar jobs. But beyond all of this are changing values and demographic patterns. The surge of female independence is certainly both a cause and effect of increased female employment. Further, today's average woman, as compared to a decade or two ago, marries earlier and bears her last child sooner.

The continuous rise in the number and importance of working women has a very special pertinence for marketers. Evidently, the industries catering to the special needs of women are most affected, but the impact goes considerably beyond that. In the past ten years, for example, the nation's total family population grew by approximately 14 percent, but the number of families with a working wife increased some 45 percent. Such families today account for about two out of every five dollars spent by consumers. and this fraction will grow in the years to come.

The Age of Working Women

Not unexpectedly, the proportion of women who work varies considerably according to age. About one out of every two adult women under twenty-five is employed. These are young persons recently out of school, or young wives earning money in the early years of marriage. The incidence of female employment, however, drops precipitously to 44 percent in the twenty-five to thirty-four age group. At this juncture of the life cycle, most women are mothers of preschool-age children. However, by the time the average woman reaches her mid-thirties her youngest child has reached school age and she can more readily reenter the labor market. Thus, the incidence of employment is again 50 percent among women in the thirty-five to forty-four age bracket. It rises to a peak level, 54 percent, for women forty-five to fifty-four, but declines abruptly after that.

The statistics also suggest that women are prone to retire from the labor force at a somewhat earlier age than men. In part at least this can be explained by the fact that, as the family grows older and children leave home, financial requirements are less pressing and the need for the wife to work diminishes.

It is also possible that older women have greater difficulty in finding employment than their younger sisters. In any event, we find that among women fifty-five to sixty-four only about 43 percent are employed outside the home. There may also be factors other than age at work here, however. Older women on the average are not as well schooled as younger ones, and hence are often less qualified for relatively pleasant white-collar jobs.

The Presence of Children

The presence of children, and more particularly the age of the child, is an important factor in a woman's disposition to seek work. Only 29 percent of mothers with children under six are employed. This ratio, however, varies according to the husband's earnings. For example, in homes where his salary is less than $7,000 a year and a preschool age child is present, about a third of the wives are in the labor force. But in a similar family unit, where the husband's income exceeds $10,000 a year, the working wife incidence is 18 percent.

The presence of older children—those six to seventeen—appears to be a factor which encourages the woman to seek work. At almost all income levels, measured in terms of the husband's earnings only, the proportion of wives working is higher in families which include children of school age than it is in families where there is no child living at home. The difference is especially large at the lower end of the income scale, but narrows as we move into the higher brackets. In families where the husband earns over $10,000 the difference disappears.

Since jobs are more numerous in the cities, and since the suburban home is more likely to include children, it is generally assumed that a larger proportion of in-town wives are working than are suburban wives. The statistics only partially support this assumption.

It is estimated that slightly over 40 percent of all married women who live in town seek employment, while in the suburbs the figure comes to more than 37 percent. The unexpected closeness of these ratios is to be explained in part by the fact that the average married woman in town is older than the one living in the suburbs. Many couples move to the big city after the last child has left home. The important thing to note here is that the working wife is not primarily a city woman. On the contrary, more working wives live in the suburbs than in town.

However, if we include in the calculations all women, married and unmarried, the labor-force participation rate does run much higher in the city than in the suburbs—52 percent as compared with 45 percent. Since the population of the suburbs is larger than that of the cities, however, just about as many working women live in the country as in town.

Education

The more educated the woman the more likely she is to seek work. This, too, perhaps is a surprising finding, since female employment is generally associated with low income and modest schooling. The numbers, though, tell quite a different story. Only about one out of every four women with less than a full elementary school education is in the labor force, but close to one out of every two women with a high school degree works. Among women who have acquired a college degree, the participation rate is 55 percent, and it exceeds 70 percent among those who have pursued graduate study.

In some small measure we again encounter the age factor here. Relatively older women have acquired less schooling than the younger generation, and as already observed, labor-force participation rates decline sharply after fifty-five. But perhaps of greater pertinence is the fact that better educated women are more likely to be restless with housekeeping, and good schooling increases the probability of locating pleasant employment.

In any event, women who work are a good deal better schooled than those that stay at home. About 23 percent of the women in the labor force have at least some college training, while for nonworking women the ratio is a more modest 16 percent. Further, about 45 percent of all women with jobs have a high school diploma, but only 35 percent of those not employed have achieved that degree of schooling.

About one out of every three working women holds a clerical job, primarily secretarial. The second most important areas of activity are the service industries, which account for about one out of every four working women. Included here are hairdressers, nurses, hospital aides, waitresses, domestics, and the like.

About 15 percent of all women who work are in professional or technical jobs. This includes teachers and laboratory technicians. All told, about 60 percent of all working women are in white-collar pursuits, while slightly over 15 percent are blue-collar workers.

Over the years there has been a moderate change in the occupational mix of working women. The developments here roughly parallel the shift in the nation's occupational pattern. The number of women in professional and technical jobs has been increasing quite sharply, and clerical employment has also been growing rapidly. Service employment, too, has been on the rise at a faster than average rate.

Husband's Earnings

There is evidently a correlation between husband's earnings and the incidence of working wives. However, the relationship here is again less pronounced than is often assumed. In fact, at the lower end of the income scale we find that the more the husband earns the more probable it is the wife is employed. For example, last year about 40 percent of all wives married to men earning $3,000-$5,000 a year worked, while for wives married to men earning $5,000-$7,000 a year the rate was over 45 percent. But this again is to be explained by the age differences at the various earning levels. With age held constant, the incidence of working women does not differ very much at the lower levels of the income scale as defined by the husband's earnings. However, as we move above the $7,000-a-year level, the incidence of working wives does decline as the husband's earnings rise. For example, 43 percent of the wives married to men earning $7,000-$10,000 are in the labor force, but only a third where the husband earns over $10,000.

All told, about 20 percent of working wives are married to men who earn over $10,000 a year, and an additional 30 percent to those who earn $7,000-$10,000. Evidently then, a fairly large number of working wives are in homes where the husband's earnings already place the family in the middle- or upper-income brackets.

The Wife's Contribution

The proportion of total family income contributed by a working wife varies quite considerably. First, many women work only part time, while in other instances the wife's absolute contribution may be impressive, but still small in relative terms since the husband's earnings are substantial. On the average, however, it is estimated that close to 40 percent of working wives account for over a third of their family's aggregate annual income. At the lower echelons of the earning scale the wife's relative contribution tends to be somewhat larger than it is in the middle- and upper-income brackets. This reflects in part the fact that in many low-income families the husband is either unemployed or is working only part time.

The sharp escalation in the nation's income distribution curve experienced since the end of World War II can be attributed in some measure to the spreading prevalence of working wives. As we move up in the income scale—at least up to the $25,000 level—the incidence of working wives also rises. For example, among homes with earnings of less than

$5,000 a year only one out of every four wives works, while for those in the $5,000-$10,000 bracket the ratio is about one out of every three. Among families with earnings of $10,000-$25,000 one out of every two wives is employed.

This progression, of course, is to be expected since the woman's earnings increase the family's aggregate income. But what marketers should observe here is the fact that the upper-income bracket does not, as is often supposed, constitute a homogeneous market, but is made up of rather distinctly different segments.

In about half of all upper-income homes—those in the $15,000 and over bracket—the husband's earnings alone are sufficient to achieve that economic status. In all other instances, however, the contribution of a second working member, usually the wife, is necessary to sustain that level of income. We have, then, two distinctly different family situations, with presumably different life styles and spending patterns. The upper-income bracket is not, as is generally assumed, monolithic and static, but rather extensively segmented and in constant process of change.

TRENDS IN EDUCATIONAL ATTAINMENT OF WOMEN [2]

The level of education attained by women has risen steadily since the turn of the century. Secondary school education is now available to all, and access to higher education has been greatly facilitated in recent years. . . .

Another measure of the increased level of educational attainment of women and men is the rise in the proportion of the population who have completed four years or more of college. In April 1940 about 1.4 million women twenty-five years of age and over, or 3.7 percent of the woman population of that age, were college graduates . . . By March 1968 about 4.5 million women twenty-five years of age and over,

[2] From a report of the United States Labor Department's Women's Bureau. The Bureau. Washington D.C. 20210. '69. p 1-10.

or 8.0 percent of the woman population, had completed four years or more of college. Men made even better progress over the twenty-eight-year period. The number of men twenty-five years of age and over who were college graduates rose from 2.0 million in April 1940 to 6.7 million in March 1968. Moreover, the proportion of the male population of that age who had completed four years or more of college increased from 5.4 to 13.3 percent.

Following are specific trends for women by level of education:

High School Graduates

Since 1900 there has been a steady growth (with the exception of one decade) in the number of girls graduating from high school—from 57,000 in 1900 to 367,000 in 1930, to 966,000 in 1960, and to 1.4 million in 1968. The slight decline between 1940 and 1950 is attributable to the low birth rate during the depression decade of the 1930s. In 1900 only 7 per 100 girls seventeen years of age in the population graduated from high school. This ratio increased to 32 per 100 in 1930, to 67 per 100 in 1960, and to 78 per 100 in 1968. The comparable ratios for boys were 5 per 100 in 1900, 26 per 100 in 1930, 61 per 100 in 1960, and 75 per 100 in 1968.

Girls have consistently outnumbered boys among high school graduates. However, the difference in the number of girl and boy graduates has narrowed in the last few decades. High school graduating classes recently have been composed almost equally of girls and boys—50.4 and 49.6 percent, respectively, in 1968. . . .

First-Time College Enrollees

Nearly 819,000 women and more than 1.089 million men were enrolled in college for the first time in October 1968. . . . This represents an increase of 14 percent for women and 16 percent for men over the previous year's first-time enrollments, as compared with increases of 7 percent for women and 5 percent for men from 1966 to 1967. These data include first-time students in institutions of higher education both in degree-credit programs and in programs not chiefly creditable toward a bachelor's degree, and are therefore not comparable with data for 1965 and prior years.

First-time students in degree-credit programs only included 712,596 women and 931,036 men in 1968, an increase of 15 percent for women and 12 percent for men over the comparable enrollment figures for 1965. During the twenty-year period since 1948 the number of women enrolled for the first time in such programs increased 3.5 times; the number of men, 2.5 times.

First-time college enrollments, particularly of women, have increased proportionately more than high school graduations over the twenty-year period, and substantially more during the past few years for both men and women. These differences represent in part a rise in the proportions of young men and women who go on to college directly from high school. They also represent a substantial increase in the number of men and women who enter college after being out of school for a year or more.

Of all women students fourteen to thirty-four years of age enrolled in the first year of college in October 1966, 30 percent had graduated from high school before 1966 and 9 percent had graduated in 1961 or earlier. Among men first-year students, 34 percent had graduated before 1966 and 15 percent in 1961 or earlier. Among students enrolled in two-year colleges, the figures were even more striking: 43 percent of men and 36 percent of women first-year students had graduated before 1966, and 21 percent of men and 11 percent of women had graduated in 1961 or before. . . .

Bachelor's and First Professional Degrees

The increase in recent years in the number of women first-time college enrollees is now being reflected in the rising number of women receiving college degrees. Not only the number but also the proportion of all bachelor's and first professional degrees earned by women rose significantly between 1960 and 1965. This trend has continued since 1966 despite the change in definition for first professional degrees.

The number of women earning bachelor's and first professional degrees increased from little more than 5,000 in 1900 to about 49,000 in 1930, to 139,000 in 1960, and to 279,000 in 1968. Between 1900 and 1930 the rate of increase in the number of such degrees awarded was greater for women than for men—833 percent compared with 232 percent. In contrast, between 1930 and 1960 the rate of increase in degrees earned was greater for men than for women—247 percent compared with 185 percent. A return to the previous trend occurred between 1960 and 1965, when the number of degrees earned by women rose by 57 percent compared with 25 percent among men. From 1966 to 1968 the rate of increase in degrees earned was only slightly greater for women (24 percent) than for men (19 percent).

In both 1900 and 1910 women earned about 20 percent of the total bachelor's and first professional degrees. Following World War I, this proportion rose sharply to about 40 percent in 1930 and 1940. Because college graduating classes in 1950 included large numbers of World War II veterans, the proportion of such degrees earned by women declined to 24 percent. By 1965 this proportion had rebounded to 41 percent. Women earned 42 percent of the total bachelor's and first professional degrees in 1968.

Of the 278,761 bachelor's and first professional degrees earned by women in 1968, 1,645 were first professional degrees requiring six years or more of higher education. This is a 15 percent increase since 1966, the first year when separate data on first professional degrees were available on a comparable basis. Women's share of all first professional degrees awarded in 1965 and 1968 amounted to 4.5 and 4.7 percent, respectively. In contrast, women earned 42.6 percent of bachelor's degrees only in 1966, and 43.5 percent in 1968. . . .

Advanced Degrees

An increasing number and proportion of all degrees earned by both women and men have been at the master's and doctor's degree level. In 1900 only 6 percent of all degrees earned by women were at this level. By 1930 this percentage had doubled to 12. From 1950 to 1965 it averaged about 15 percent. With the change in definition, the proportion was 18 percent in 1966, and 19 percent in 1968. The trend for men was slightly different. In 1900, 7 percent of all degrees earned by men were at the advanced degree level. This percentage rose to 13 in 1930 and to 15 in 1940, but dropped to 12 in 1950 when the number of men receiving bachelor's and first professional degrees reached a peak after World War II. It rose to 22 percent in 1965 and to 25 percent in 1966 and 1968.

Master's Degrees: About three hundred women earned master's degrees in 1900. A momentous expansion ocurred between that date and 1930 when 6,000 women earned master's degrees—a twenty-fold increase. From 1930 to 1960 the rate of growth in the number of women earning master's degrees was considerable but did not match this earlier advance. The rate of increase accelerated between 1960 and 1965 and amounted to 53 percent; during the two-year period from 1966 to 1968 it amounted to a striking 33 percent. Among men the rate of growth from 1900 to 1960 was more even—from 1,300 in 1900 to 8,900 in 1930, and to 51,000 in 1960. As was true for women, the rate of increase in the number of master's degrees earned by men accelerated between 1960 and 1965 and amounted to 50 percent. But the rate of growth for men from 1966 to 1968 (22 percent) was considerably less than for women. More than 63,000 women and nearly 114,000 men earned master's degrees in 1968.

In 1900 women accounted for about 20 percent of all master's degree recipients. By 1930 this proportion had grown to 40 percent. In 1950, despite the increase in the number of women earning master's degrees, their share of all master's degrees earned had dropped to 29 percent. After that a slight recovery occurred, and the proportion of all master's degrees earned by women had leveled off at about 32 percent in 1965. Between 1966 and 1968, after the change in definition, it increased from 34 to 36 percent.

Doctor's Degrees: The trend among women earning doctor's degrees has been similar to that for women earning master's degrees. The greatest growth in the number of women earning doctor's degrees occurred between 1900 and 1930—from 23 to 353, or a fifteen-fold increase. The rise from 1930 to 1960 was less dramatic and relatively steady. But between 1960 and 1968, the number of doctor's degrees earned by women almost tripled—from 1,028 to 2,906. Among men the rise in the number earning these degrees was more regular throughout the 1900-1960 period. Between 1960 and 1968, however, the rate of increase in doctor's degrees earned by men was less than for women—129 percent as compared with 183 percent. Men earned 360 doctor's degrees in 1900, 1,950 in 1930, 8,800 in 1960, and 20,000 in 1968.

Women earned 6 percent of all doctor's degrees in 1900. By 1920 this proportion had reached a peak of 15 percent. Since then women have earned relatively fewer doctorates— the proportion dropped to a low of 10 percent in 1950 and has risen steadily since to 13 percent in 1968.

EDUCATION AND JOBS [3]

There is a direct relationship between the educational attainment of women and their labor-force participation. The more education a woman has received, the greater the likelihood she will be engaged in paid employment. For example, in March 1968, 71 percent of women who had completed five years or more of college were in the labor force. Similarly, 54 percent of women with four years of college were employed or looking for work. The proportion

[3] From *Trends in Educational Attainment of Women,* a report of the United States Labor Department's Women's Bureau. The Bureau. Washington D.C. 20210. '69. p 10-11.

dropped to 48 percent for women high school graduates and to 24 percent for women with less than eight years of schooling. The chances of being employed were even slimmer for those women who had less than five years of formal education.

This pattern of greater labor-force participation among women with higher educational attainment generally held true when the figures were broken down by age group. Exceptionally high labor-force participation rates were shown for both women forty-five to fifty-four years of age with five years or more of college (86 percent) and women twenty to twenty-four years of age with four years of college (82 percent). Among women with less than eight years of schooling, labor-force participation rates were generally below 40 percent. Exceptions were the very small group of young women eighteen and nineteen years old with a rate of 40 percent, and women thirty-five to fifty-four years of age with 41 percent in the labor force.

Educational attainment appears to exert a stronger influence today on whether a woman works than it did in October 1952. The labor-force participation rate of all women eighteen years of age and over increased 6.4 percentage points to 42 percent from October 1952 to March 1968. For those with a high school education or better, however, the increase was 7.4 percentage points or more. On the other hand, the labor-force participation rates of women with eight years or less of schooling were practically unchanged over the same period, except for a decline from 28 to 17 percent among those with less than five years of formal education.

This growth in labor-force participation among women with the most education and the reduction in the likelihood of employment among women with relatively little schooling generally are sustained when comparisons are made by age group over the seventeen-year period. The extent of the increase or decrease, of course, varied somewhat among the age groups. The greatest increase in labor-force participation of women college graduates was shown by those twenty-five to thirty-four years of age. The decrease in labor-force participation of women with less than five years of schooling was most noticeable among those under thirty-five years of age.

JOB BIAS AGAINST WOMEN
EASING UNDER PRESSURE [4]

Even the Lord, according to the Old Testament, figured a woman's effort was worth less.

"If it is a male from twenty to sixty years of age, the equivalent is fifty shekels of silver by the sanctuary weight; if it is a female, the equivalent is thirty shekels," He told Moses in Leviticus 27:3 and 4.

And that is still the scale; a few thousand years later American women still average about 60 percent of men's pay.

But the walls of economic and psychological discrimination against women in the American job market are beginning to crack under the pressures of the Federal Governmen, the Women's Liberation movement and the efforts of thousands of individual women themselves.

The barriers may never come down completely; many women consider themselves short-timers in the job market, not lifers, and don't mind not being considered for better paying jobs. But for those who do mind, the cracks in the wall are visible and widening almost every day. For example:

The Supreme Court [has] ruled . . . that women may not be excluded from jobs because they have children unless men are too. The decision points toward the day when women may receive a constitutional right to such equal job treatment, one of the goals of the equal rights amendment that failed in the last Congress. . . .

Federal authorities have begun acting against universities charged with discriminating against women, using the threat to withhold Federal contracts as a lever. . . .

[4] From article by Jerry M. Flint, staff correspondent. New York *Times*. p 1. Ja. 31, '71. © 1971 by The New York Times Company. Reprinted by permission.

The number of complaints by women to Government agencies about discrimination is growing. The Labor Department reports that violation charges involving equal pay laws increased 91 percent in the last fiscal year over 1969 and that back-pay awards are up 2.5 times, spurred by information programs around the nation informing women of their job and pay rights.

Protection Under Law

Today, women have some job protection under the Civil Rights Act of 1964, from the Equal Employment Opportunities Commission, from the Fair Labor Standards Act barring pay discrimination in factory jobs, and from an executive order of October 1967, barring such discrimination by Government contractors.

Discrimination at universities, for example, is susceptible to Government action because many of the schools hold Government contracts. But most of these acts have some loopholes that allow discrimination against women for one reason or another.

Women's groups have criticized the Government, particularly the Justice Department, for failure to fight harder for women's job equality. In December [1970], the Justice Department settled its first suit against such job discrimination against the Libbey-Owens-Ford Glass Company with a consent decree, but women complained that a demand for back pay had been dropped.

If Government has not acted as effectively as women wanted in the past, however, the HEW [Department of Health, Education, and Welfare] action with universities and the Labor Department activity show that the pace has stepped up.

The ordinary type of prejudice against hiring women or giving them equal pay "is rapidly diminishing," said Laurence Silberman, Under Secretary of Labor. "It seems to fall down when you simply push it." The "shared premise that women are not seriously in the work force, that they are the dilettantes in the work force," he said, is fairly easy to dispel today.

Women themselves—there are 30.1 million in the labor force, including factory workers, college graduates, housewives, most of them unconnected with any formal "liberation" movement—are speaking up angrily:

"Whenever you see a man on the job, that's the easiest job," said Mrs. Ethel Wargnier, an auto worker in Detroit.

"I Want My Own Secretary"

"Oh, Miss Sloan, how fast do you type?" That, says Marjorie Sloan, twenty-three years old, is the kind of question she is asked at job interviews. "After five years of college I want my own secretary when I get a job," she said. Her best job to date: modeling her feet at $25 an hour.

There is no doubt that discrimination exists.

"The fact that men earn more than women is one of the best established and least satisfactorily explained aspects of American labor-market behavior," said Victor Fuchs, a City University of New York professor and vice president in charge of research for the National Bureau of Economic Research. "This cannot be explained by inherent differences in ability."

Government reports for 1968 show the median full-time earnings of white men at $7,396, of Negro men at $4,777, of white women at $4,279, and of Negro women at $3,194. Women with some college education, both white and black, earn less than Negro men with eight years of education, a special presidential committee reported.

A Middle-Class Revolt

The earnings gap spreads throughout a wide spectrum of jobs. For women salesworkers, full time in 1968, the median wage was $3,461, while for men it was $8,549; for professional workers it was $6,691 against $10,151. Full university professors, women, were earning $11,649; men got $12,768. Chemists were earning $9,000 if they were women,

$13,500 if they were men. Only 3 percent of working women earn more than $10,000 a year, against 28 percent for men.

In work areas where a large part of the work force is female, women tend to be in the lower- paying jobs. In medicine, for example, women are nurses, men are doctors; at the telephone company, women are switchboard operators; at supermarkets, women are checkout clerks.

One reason why the job discrimination problem is under attack today is that the number of college-educated, middle-class women is increasing. The middle-class "always has been the leader in any revolution," said a woman official of the Labor Department. "In the black movement it was the NAACP, not the welfare mothers, that led."

Another reason is that there are more and more divorced women in the work force requiring an income to support a family, as well as more and more working wives.

"I went to my high school reunion in Missouri," recalled Representative Martha Griffiths [Republican, Michigan], a political champion of the woman's cause, "and the first three women I talked to, all their children were divorced. Women my age didn't work, but they knew their daughters would have to work." ...

Women easily apply the rhetoric of the black civil rights movement to their own circumstances, but their job troubles seem far different from those of the blacks. Women, for example, are not a minority but a majority in the nation: As of July 1969, there were 103.4 million women in the United States and 99.8 million men. Women also have high educational levels and control a vast amount of wealth.

Some insist the job trouble is not really what is normally called discrimination by employers. Most of the difference in pay, says Professor Fuchs "can be explained by the different roles assigned to men and women in our society. Role differentiation, which begins in the cradle, affects the choice of occupation, labor force attachment, location of work, post-school investment, hours of work, and other variables that influence earnings."

Women are taking note of this "role assignment." A housewife watching a TV news show recently shouted, "Look! We're being programmed!" She was reacting to what would have passed as a simple scene a few years ago: a small boy told the TV reporter he would like to be a doctor, and the reporter turned to a nearby girl, no more than seven years old, and asked, "What about you, would you like to be his nurse?"

Catherine East of the Labor Department said: "Psychologically it's easier for a woman to cop out than a man, to give up and quit." A man is expected to stick to his job even if fed up, she said, "but society will say a woman's doing the right thing when she quits."

Mr. Silberman said: "Women must make the psychological shift themselves—to an attitude of 'I want to be in the work force, a doctor, a lawyer.' Then it will be done." A substantial psychological change is taking place, he said, "but some haven't made the psychological shifts."

Even factory women are likely to complain just as much about the attitudes of other women as of men. "Our women never went into skilled trades programs—they seemed to be afraid even to try," said Mrs. Dorothy Walker, who works at a General Motors plant in Ypsilanti, Michigan.

Younger, More Pushy

"The younger women are more pushy," said Miss Betty Mickens, a Ford worker and an officer in a United Auto Workers local. "They sign up for the better jobs. If the foreman says anything about it they'll look at him like he's crazy."

"These younger women will not take what the older women will take," said Miss Bernice Shields, another Ford worker.

But there is evidence of outright discrimination, too. Jack Shingleton, director of Michigan State University's employment bureau, reports, for example, that most companies say they pay the same salaries to women and men graduates but "limited salary data does not bear this out" except in a few professions.

When asked why they are paying women less, Mr. Shingleton said, he gets such answers as: Traditionally they are paid less; they will take less; they haven't the skills to compete with men or the mobility of men; they are working for a short time.

"There are gradual changes taking place in the area of employment of women," he said, "but as in any problem where discrimination is a big factor, changes come slowly." ...

Many Put Husband First

There is no question that many and perhaps most women are not looking for careers when they go to work. In talks with dozens of women, few said they expected to be working all their lives. Some expected to work a few years, until they were married or until they had helped to pay for something —a house, say, or furniture.

Miss Sloan, who is angry because after five years of college she is still being asked to be a secretary, also conceded that her allegiance would be to a future husband. "I know I'm not going to have that much ambition, to make $100,000," she said. "I'll get married, and after that it will depend on my husband's wishes."

Professor Fuchs said his study showed that "never-married women, who are much more likely to stay in the labor force and who have more incentive to invest in themselves after formal schooling is completed, have an 'age earnings profile' which is very similar to that of men."

Nevertheless, practically every woman interviewed said she felt that at some time in her working career she had been discriminated against, held back or paid less because of her sex.

Mrs. Stella Deakin, a Detroit factory worker, said: "Whenever they asked to be upgraded into better jobs, they [meaning other men, company or union] put obstacles in your way."

And Representative Griffiths said: "When my husband and I graduated from law school we went to work for the same insurance company. We did the same work, and he was paid $10 a week more. We were mad." And she still is.

WOMEN'S JOB RIGHTS GAIN IN FEDERAL COURT RULINGS [5]

Federal courts across the nation have unloosed a stream of decisions in recent months that appear to be on their way toward wiping out all state laws that prohibit women from working in certain types of jobs, and that limit their hours of work and decrease their opportunities for promotions.

Recent decisions of various Federal courts in the area of employment-rights of women are also doing the following things:

Limiting the one legal basis for sex discrimination by private employers under the Civil Rights Act of 1964— the concept that sex can be a "bona fide occupational qualification" for some jobs.

Rendering invalid employer requirements that women employees in certain jobs remain unmarried and, in two out of three cases so far tried, invalidating state laws and employer rules that require women to retire at a certain point in pregnancy.

Holding employers liable for awards of back pay to women who were kept from working overtime or denied employment in better-paid job classifications because of their sex.

None of these cases has yet reached the Supreme Court, and lawyers who are active in the women's rights field concede it is possible that the Court could reverse or limit some of the lower court decisions in cases involving marriage, pregnancy, back pay and occupational qualifications.

What are generally termed the state "protective" laws

[5] From article by Eileen Shanahan, staff correspondent. New York *Times.* p 1. Jl. 13, '71. © 1971 by The New York Times Company. Reprinted by permission.

are a different matter, however. Women's rights lawyers, even those who represent employers, generally feel there is no doubt that protective laws are going to be held invalid.

That is because the lower courts, in what is now more than a dozen cases, have been unanimous in invalidating these laws, which limit the hours during which women may work, set maximum weights they may lift on the job, and in some states, ban their employment in such occupations as mining.

A number of Federal district courts and the United States Court of Appeals for the Ninth Circuit have held that these laws conflict with Title VII of the Civil Rights Act of 1964 and that the Federal law takes precedence. Title VII prohibits discrimination in hiring and in job assignments on the basis of sex, race, color, religion or national origin.

Some women's rights lawyers believe that the issue of state protective laws may never reach the Supreme Court, because most employers do not appeal once they have lost a sex discrimination case through invalidation of a state law that they were obeying. The first such case to reach even the Court of Appeals level was decided only last month [June 1971].

The prospective elimination of all the protective laws may have an impact on the prospects for enactment of the pending equal rights amendment to the Constitution, which would bar sex discrimination through any action of a government.

Advocates of the amendment believe the amendment would still be needed, even if all the protective laws are eliminated, because otherwise there is no way to force states to end sex discrimination in their property and family-relations laws, or to end sex discrimination by state university systems.

The opponents of the equal rights amendment, including a number of unions and some women labor leaders, have based their opposition largely on the argument that working-class women needed the protection against exploitation by employers that the state laws provided.

If the state laws are eliminated anyway, that argument against the amendment would disappear.

Most of the cases that have resulted in invalidation of the various state laws were brought by working-class women who contended that, whatever the original intent of these laws, they kept women from earning premium overtime and nightshift pay that they wanted to earn, kept them out of better-paid job classifications and prevented their promotion to such jobs as foreman.

Different Views

In situations where state laws were not an issue, different Federal courts have taken different views of the extent to which an employer may refuse to hire one sex or the other for certain jobs in the belief that only one sex could perform well at the job. But three different recent decisions would sharply limit an employer's right to claim that sex was a "bona fide occupational qualification" for a job—a "B.F.O.Q.," as it is known.

The strongest of the three recent cases, *Diaz v. Pan American World Airways,* involves a man who wanted to be assigned as a steward on a Pan American route that uses only stewardesses. The airline argued that passengers on this type of flight preferred women as airplane cabin attendants, and that strong consumer preference constituted a B.F.O.Q.

The United States Court of Appeals for the Fifth Circuit ruled, however, that "discrimination based on sex is valid only when the essence of the business operation would be undermined" by the failure to hire one sex exclusively.

In another case, *Weeks v. Southern Bell,* involving a woman who wanted a job as a switchman with a telephone company, the United States Court of Appeals for the Ninth Circuit held that the employer had the burden of proving that substantially all women could not perform the job safely and efficiently.

In another case, *Rosenfeld v. Southern Pacific*, involving a woman who wanted to be a railroad agent, the United States Court of Appeals for the Ninth Circuit held that a woman must be given the opportunity to prove she could do the job.

David W. Zugswerdt, a top trial lawyer at the Equal Employment Opportunity Commission, which has been involved in many of the woman's employment rights suits, believes that these three cases virtually eliminate the B.F.O.Q. exception from the 1964 Civil Rights Law.

But N. Thompson Powers, a former executive director of the commission who now has a private law practice here, disagrees. He has defended some employers in women's rights cases, and he notes that, in the only case involving alleged sex discrimination in employment that has thus far reached the Supreme Court, the Court kept open the determination of what constituted a B.F.O.Q.

That was the case of *Phillips v. the Martin Marietta Corporation*. The Court held that the company's rule against hiring women with preschool-age children was a violation of the 1964 Civil Rights Act. But the Court also returned the case to the trial court to determine whether parenthood, "if demonstrably more relevant to job performance for a woman than for a man," could be bona fide occupational qualification—or disqualification, in this instance.

Women's rights activists are particularly pleased with one of the two cases they won recently in Federal district courts, invalidating requirements that women take leave from their job at a certain point in their pregnancy.

In *Cohen v. the Chesterfield County School Board*, the Federal District Court in Richmond held that the mandatory maternity-leave requirement violated the Fourteenth Amendment's guarantee of equal protection of the laws to all persons.

The decision was one of the few in which a Federal court has held that the Fourteenth Amendment applies to women. The Supreme Court has explicitly held to the con-

trary numerous times. Many of the discriminations that
women's rights activists are trying to overcome would be
illegal if the Supreme Court would apply the Fourteenth
Amendment to women.

Two other cases involving enforced maternity leave—one
in Texas upholding the woman and the other in Ohio upholding the mandatory-leave rule—are pending before
United States Courts of Appeals.

A final major area of recent court action in cases involving women's employment rights concerns the award of back
pay to women who have been discriminated against.

$30 Million Awarded

Two laws are involved: the 1964 Civil Rights Act and
the 1963 Equal Pay Act.

The precedent-setting case under the Equal Pay Act, the
Wheaton Glass Company case, held that the work performed
must be only "substantially equal" work, not necessarily
identical.

Since that case was decided last year, scores of equal pay
cases have been filed and more than $30 million in back
pay has been awarded by courts since the beginning of this
year. Back pay awards under the Equal Pay Act are limited
to two years.

Under the Civil Rights Act, claims for back pay generally
arise from charges that women were not permitted to hold
jobs in highly paid categories, or that they were denied overtime in a discriminatory fashion.

Plaintiffs in back pay cases under the Civil Rights Act
of 1954 are trying to establish that the liability for retroactive pay goes back to the enactment of the statute. Attorneys for the defendants contend that the liability goes
back only ninety days before the charge of discrimination
was filed.

Mr. Zugswerdt of the Equal Employment Opportunity
Commission says that employers should be on notice that
their "potential liability is absolutely staggering" under the

1964 act. But he adds that most employers can probably avoid suits that could result in big back-pay awards if they stop discriminatory hiring and promotion practices now.

STATUS OF WOMEN [6]

It is a mistake to judge the strength of the new rise of feminism by the relatively small number of women who physically storm male sanctuaries or shout obscenities at male reporters. They are only the outer edge of mounting impatience among women against the secondary role which society has assigned to their sex. Like the Black Panther Party in its relationship to the Negro population, the few militant women awaken deeply buried feelings within large numbers of other women who never before consciously thought of themselves as oppressed.

Women's rights as an issue has rarely interested more than a handful of men, except as a subject for humor. Its resurgence at this time, however, may well herald a considerable change in the American life style affecting men and women alike—certainly more change than followed suffrage a half-century ago. Some observers believe the impact will be even greater than that of the black drive for status. The male editor of the *Ladies' Home Journal*, John Mack Carter, whose office was invaded March 18, 1970, by two hundred feminists to voice their complaints about the contents of women's magazines, wrote later that "beneath the shrill accusations and the radical dialectic, our editors heard some convincing truths about the persistence of sexual discrimination." In an introduction to a special section of the August issue of the *Journal* which he turned over to the protesting women, Carter said: "We seemed to catch a rising note of angry self-expression among today's American women, a desire for representation, for recognition, for a broadening range of alternatives in a rapidly changing society."

[6] From a report by Helen B. Shaffer, staff writer. *Editorial Research Reports.* p 565-72. Ag. 5, '70. Reprinted by permission.

The new movement "may have an impact far beyond its extremist eccentricities."

Advisory boards to the Federal Government have taken note of the growing feminist fury. Virginia R. Allen, chairman of the President's Task Force on Women's Rights and Responsibilities, told President Nixon: "American women are increasingly aware and restive over the denial of equal opportunity, equal responsibility, equal protection of law." The Citizen's Advisory Council on the Status of Women observed that "a revival of the feminist movement has occurred during the past four years and it is greatly increasing in momentum, especially among younger women."

The new awareness and restiveness of women have been heightened by social unrest and the sexual revolution. Today's feminists are a different breed from their sisters who fought for suffrage. They do not limit themselves to specific goals such as equality in employment. They are mounting an assault on an entrenched pattern of relations between the sexes that, in their eyes, demeans and restricts one half the human race. It follows that feminist militants are in the vanguard of opposition to abortion laws which they consider a denial of a woman's control over her own body. They are for abolition of alimony for wife support if a divorcée is physically and mentally able to support herself. They are in arms against mass media presentation of women as sexual objects; some Women's Lib groups are calling for a boycott of products of companies that stress female sexual allure in their advertising. At the extreme, they oppose conventional marriage in favor of "voluntary association": motherhood without a husband would become fully acceptable.

New Activist Groups; Discrimination Complaints

Though only a very few women publicly protest their "second sex" status and millions of women obviously have no desire to abandon their traditional role as wife-mother-homemaker, there are signs nevertheless that pressures for equalization are moving forward. For one thing, feminine activism is bringing concrete results. Individual women, often backed by militant feminist organizations, are filing formal complaints against employers, unions, educational institutions, restaurants, and Government agencies, charging discrimination against members of their sex. Three relatively new organizations have been particularly effective in bringing pressure on regulatory bodies to act on sex discrimination complaints and in initiating or supporting litigation in the field of women's rights. They are NOW [National Organization of Women], founded in 1966 by Betty Friedan, author of *The Feminine Mystique,* and the still newer WEAL (Women's Equity Action League) and Human Rights for Women, Inc.

NOW, based in New York, has thirty-five chapters around the country and claims 5,000 to 10,000 members. It appeals to discontented housewives as well as to working women and is the nearest thing to a mass organization the new feminism has produced. WEAL is made up chiefly of professional and business women and works largely in the field of legal action. Human Rights for Women, based in Washington, D.C., supplies legal aid in sex discrimination cases. These are traditionally structured organizations with specific goals to be obtained by working within the political system. In addition there are more radical groups, spawned by the New Left and the campus protest movements, which come and go under a variety of names. The best-known among them are Women's Liberation, the Radical Feminists, WITCH (Women's International Terrorist Conspiracy from Hell) and Redstockings.

Knocking down sex barriers to men's bars may not at first sight seem a great boon to the welfare of womankind. But to the women who brought suit against McSorley's Old Ale House in New York, the victory in court provided the satisfaction of laying down a principle. A Federal judge ruled on June 25, 1970, that McSorley's, an all-male tavern since its founding in 1854, was a public place subject to the equal protection clause of the Constitution, and hence its exclusion of women customers was unconstitutional. While the ruling was on appeal to higher court, the New York City Council on July 22 enacted an ordinance to prohibit discrimination against women in bars, restaurants, and similar public places. To women of the Liberation movement, segregation by sex is like segregation by race—a form of discrimination, damaging economically, socially, and psychologically. And there are many "men only" signs, seen and unseen, that block a woman's way to a good lunch—or a promotion.

Of more immediate benefit to the cause may be the feminist drive against discrimination in employment, which has begun to show results. Approximately one fourth of the 12,000 charges of discrimination in employment brought before the Equal Employment Opportunity Commission each year involve discrimination because of sex. The commission administers Title VII of the Civil Rights Act of 1964, which forbids discrimination in employment on account of race, color, religion, national origin, or sex. Under feminist pressure, the commission toughened its stand on the employment rights of women. It voted August 15, 1969, to amend its guidelines so that employers cannot be excused for practices unlawful under the Federal Act by claiming that those practices conform with state laws. Paradoxically, many of those state laws were enacted originally to protect women in such matters as long hours, night work and physically difficult work. The commission said such laws "have ceased to be relevant to our technology or to the expanding role of the female worker in our economy."

Federal courts in California and Oregon ruled in 1968 and 1969 that state laws protecting women workers were superseded by the sex-discrimination ban in Title VII. Attorneys general in at least six states—Michigan, North Dakota, Oklahoma, Ohio, Pennsylvania and South Dakota—and the Corporation Counsel of the District of Columbia have issued similar opinions in recent months. In several cases the employing firm has taken the initiative in suits to throw out laws limiting women's hours of work.

The United States Court of Appeals for the Seventh Circuit (Chicago) ruled on September 26, 1969, that employers may not exclude women from jobs requiring the lifting of thirty-five pounds or more, but must afford each worker "a reasonable opportunity to demonstrate his or her ability to perform more strenuous jobs." In a similar case the Fifth Circuit Court of Appeals (New Orleans) held that the burden of proof lies on the employer to prove he had "a factual basis for believing that . . . substantially all women would be unable to perform safely and efficiently the duties of the job involved."

Tightening of Federal Rules to Prevent Job Bias

The Equal Employment Opportunity Commission has taken the position that employers and employment agencies cannot advertise a preference for one sex or the other unless sex is a "bona fide occupational qualification." Such jobs are said to be very few—jobs for actors and washroom attendants perhaps but not nurses or engineers or stewards of ships or planes. The commission issued a guideline on January 24, 1969, holding it unlawful to place ads in "Help Wanted—Male" or "Help Wanted—Female" columns unless sex is genuinely a "B.F.O.Q." The American Newspaper Publishers Association and the Washington (D.C.) *Evening Star* have challenged this rule in a court case. Many newspapers have continued the custom of sex-separated Help Wanted columns. Only recently have individual women, moved by the new feminist fervor, begun to file charges on the want-ad question.

The Supreme Court in March 1970 decided to review its first case involving a charge of sex discrimination in employment under the 1964 Civil Rights Act. At issue is the validity of a company rule that excluded a mother of young children from a position as assembly-line trainee. The Court will review an appeal from a lower Federal court decision favorable to the company, Martin Marietta Corporation. The case is of particular interest because G. Harrold Carswell voted with the majority of judges in appellate court who denied a petition for rehearing. When President Nixon later nominated Carswell for the Supreme Court, feminists remembered his vote and accused him of being a "sexist." Representative Patsy T. Mink (Democrat, Hawaii) was among several women who testified against his nomination at Senate Judiciary Committee hearings. The Senate on April 8, 1970, rejected the Carswell nomination, but not on grounds of "sexism."

Complaints of violations of the Equal Pay Act of 1963 rose from 351 in 1965 to approximately 565 in fiscal 1970. According to the Department of Labor, which administers this law, an estimated $17 million in back pay is due women workers who have been paid less than men for the same work, contrary to law. The Supreme Court laid down an important principle recently in an equal pay case involving female employees of the Wheaton Glass Company of Millville, New Jersey—that jobs need not be identical but only "substantially equal" for the equal pay rule to apply. A Federal district court in Dallas ruled on October 8, 1969, that the traditionally all-male job of hospital orderly was substantially equal to that of the traditionally female job of nurse's aide.

The Department of Justice filed suit on July 20, 1970, against Libbey-Owens-Ford, glass manufacturer, for allegedly discriminating against women in violation of the equal employment provision of the Civil Rights Act. The department asked the United States District Court in Toledo, Ohio, to order the company to hire, train, promote, and pay women equally with men in its five Toledo area plants. Despite this landmark action—the first time the Justice Department has gone to court to enforce the sex equality provision—women leaders are critical of alleged foot-dragging by the Nixon Administration.

They were cheered on June 10, 1970, when Secretary of Labor James D. Hodgson met feminist demands by releasing guidelines for enforcing executive orders to prohibit sex discrimination by Government contractors. The guidelines directed employers not to make any distinction by sex in hiring, wages, hours, or other conditions of employment: in advertising not to specify male or female help unless sex was a bona fide job requirement; not to exclude mothers of young children (unless they also excluded the fathers), not to penalize women who took time off for childbirth, and so on. But disillusionment soon set in. At the insistence of leaders of women's rights groups, Hodgson met with them on July 25 to explain his position. Saying that discrimination against women was "subtle and more pervasive" than against any other group, he added that he had "no intention of applying literally exactly the same approach for women" as for other instances of discrimination in employment. One of the women leaders, Dr. Ann Scott of Williamsville, New York, said after the meeting: "Women have been left out again by the Nixon Administration."

Women won a partial victory, however. Hodgson announced on July 31 that "goals and timetables" would be set for employment of women by Federal contractors. The goals and timetables were to be determined after the Government had consulted with representatives of employers, labor unions, and women's groups. A blanket application of a no-discrimination rule on all jobs was not contemplated. The sex-discrimination problem differed from that of race discrimination, Hodgson said, because many women do not seek employment and many jobs sought by minority males do not attract women.

Attack on Male Favoritism in Colleges, Churches

Feminist organizations are beginning to use Federal antidiscrimination laws to attack long-standing practices of sex discrimination in higher education. The prevalence of Government-contract work in universities gives the militants a handle for bringing pressure. Favoritism toward males in hiring faculty members and admitting students to graduate and professional schools henceforth might mean the loss of a Government contract. Two of the new women's organizations, NOW and WEAL, have taken the lead here. They have named at least one hundred colleges and universities in making complaints to Federal agencies that administer the university contracts. The *Chronicle of Higher Education* reported in its issue of June 1, 1970, that Government investigators had gone to Harvard and several other campuses. Some institutions—the University of Chicago is one—have responded to rising feminist pressure by setting up investigating committees of their own.

Not all of the push is coming from new militant groups. The eighty-eight-year-old American Association of University Women has brought a complaint against the United States Office of Education for failing—despite frequent pleas—to show sex differentials in faculty rank and pay when collecting and analyzing data in higher education. The need is great for "objective data to support what we know is flagrant discrimination against women in academia," AAUW representative Ruth M. Oltman told *Editorial Research Reports*. The President's task force had made a similar recommendation. In the course of a recent survey, the association itself uncovered several hundred case histories of sex discrimination in higher education and hundreds more of job discrimination against educated women.

Women are ignoring St. Paul's admonition that they "keep silence in the churches." They are demanding—and to some degree, getting—their "rights" in leading American religious groups. Women delegates warned the American Baptist Convention in May 1970 that they would demand a woman be named president at the following year's meeting. The National Council of Churches in December 1969 chose its first woman president, Cynthia Wedel. The Lutheran Church in America yielded to feminist pressure by changing its bylaws on June 29, 1970, to permit women to become ordained ministers. Approximately one fourth of the 235 member churches of the World Council of Churches ordain women. Some orders of Roman Catholic nuns have adopted secular practices to avoid submission to the church's "male mystique." Perhaps most extraordinary of all, a girl is studying to become a rabbi at a Hebrew seminary in Cincinnati.

III. SOME PERSPECTIVES—SOCIAL AND HISTORICAL

EDITOR'S INTRODUCTION

Is the position a woman occupies in America today so very different from that of a woman a hundred or even a thousand years ago here or elsewhere? Should it be? To put some of the current ferment into perspective, this section looks both backward in time and outward from the United States.

Opening the section is a declaration issued by the United Nations General Assembly in 1967 on the rights of women. A reading of its provisions offers excellent insights into the long catalog of areas such as property ownership, custody of children, and voting rights, in which women in many parts of the world have occupied distinctly inferior legal status. Next, a comparison of the two Germanies shows that even in a socialist society which claims to favor sex equality, men are still somehow more equal.

Literary critic Richard Gilman offers a perceptive historical survey that shows how throughout history patriarchy has been the rule, even when inheritance rights passed through female lines. Subordination of women, he finds, is a thoroughly entrenched part of human social history. Gilman ends his article with a statement by John Stuart Mill's wife that stands well as a definition of what today's feminist is still fighting for. "We deny the right," Harriet Mill wrote, "of any portion of the species to decide for another portion, or any individual for another individual, what is and what is not their 'proper sphere.' A proper sphere for all human beings is the largest and highest which they are able to attain to."

Finally, Jack Rosenthal of the New York *Times* checks some early findings of the 1970 census to see if women are gaining in their quest for equality. He finds the answer to be affirmative.

U.N. DECLARATION ON WOMEN'S RIGHTS [1]

The General Assembly,

Considering that the peoples of the United Nations have, in the Charter, reaffirmed their faith in fundamental human rights, in the dignity and worth of the human person and in the equal rights of men and women,

Considering that the Universal Declaration of Human Rights asserts the principle of nondiscrimination and proclaims that all human beings are born free and equal in dignity and rights and that everyone is entitled to all the rights and freedoms set forth therein, without distinction of any kind, including any distinction as to sex,

Taking into account the resolutions, declarations, conventions and recommendations of the United Nations and the specialized agencies designed to eliminate all forms of discrimination and to promote equal rights for men and women,

Concerned that, despite the Charter, the Universal Declaration of Human Rights, International Covenants on Human Rights and other instruments of the United Nations and the specialized agencies and despite the progress made in the matter of equality of rights, there continues to exist considerable discrimination against women,

Considering that discrimination against women is incompatible with human dignity, and with the welfare of the family and of society, prevents their participation on equal terms with men, in the political, social, economic and cultural life of their countries, and is an obstacle to the full development of the potentialities of women in the service of their countries and of humanity,

[1] United Nations declaration on discrimination against women, adopted November 7, 1967. Text from New York *Times.* p 24. N. 8, '67.

Bearing in mind the great contribution made by women to social, political, economic and cultural life and the part they play in the family and particularly in the rearing of children,

Convinced that the full and complete development of a country, the welfare of the world and the cause of peace require the maximum participation of women as well as men in all fields,

Considering that it is necessary to insure the universal recognition in law and in fact of the principle of equality of men and women,

Solemnly proclaims this Declaration:

Article 1

Discrimination against women, denying or limiting as it does their equality of rights with men, is fundamentally unjust and constitutes an offense against human dignity.

Article 2

All appropriate measures shall be taken to abolish existing laws, customs, regulations and practices which are discriminatory against women, and to establish adequate legal protection for equal rights of men and women, in particular:

(a) The principle of equality of rights shall be embodied in the constitution or otherwise guaranteed by law;

(b) The international instruments of the United Nations and the specialized agencies relating to the elimination of discrimination against women shall be ratified or acceded to and fully implemented as soon as practicable.

Article 3

All appropriate measures shall be taken to educate public opinion and direct national aspirations toward the eradication of prejudice and the abolition of customary and all other practices which are based on the idea of the inferiority of women.

Article 4

All appropriate measures shall be taken to ensure to women on equal terms with men without any discrimination:

(a) The right to vote in all elections and be eligible for election to all publicly elected bodies;

(b) The right to vote in all public referenda;

(c) The right to hold public office and to exercise all public functions.

Such rights shall be guaranteed by legislation.

Article 5

Women shall have the same rights as men to acquire, change or retain their nationality. Marriage to an alien shall not automatically affect the nationality of the wife either by rendering her stateless or by forcing on her the nationality of her husband.

Article 6

1. Without prejudice to the safeguarding of the unity and the harmony of the family, which remains the basic unit of any society, all appropriate measures, particularly legislative measures, shall be taken to insure to women, married or unmarried, equal rights with men in the field of civil law, and in particular:

(a) The right to acquire, administer and enjoy, dispose of and inherit property, including property acquired during the marriage;

(b) The right to equality in legal capacity and the exercise thereof;

(c) The same rights as men with regard to the law on the movement of persons.

2. All appropriate measures shall be taken to insure the principle of equality of status of the husband and wife, and in particular:

(a) Women shall have the same right as men to free choice of a spouse and to enter into marriage only with their free and full consent;

(b) Women shall have equal rights with men during marriage and at its dissolution. In all cases the interest of the child shall be paramount;

(c) Parents shall have equal rights and duties in matters relating to their children. In all cases the interest of the children shall be paramount.

3. Child marriage and the betrothal of young girls before puberty shall be prohibited, and effective action, including legislation, shall be taken to specify a minimum age for marriage and to make the registration of marriages in an official registry compulsory.

Article 7

All provisions of penal codes which constitute discrimination against women shall be repealed.

Article 8

All appropriate measures, including legislation, shall be taken to combat all forms of traffic in women and exploitation of prostitution of women.

Article 9

All appropriate measures shall be taken to insure to girls and women, married or unmarried, equal rights with men in education at all levels, and in particular:

(a) Equal conditions of access to, and study in, educational institutions of all types, including universities, vocational, technical and professional schools;

(b) The same choice of curricula, the same examinations, teaching staff with qualifications of the same standard, and school premises and equipment of the same quality, whether the institutions are coeducational or not;

(c) Equal opportunities to benefit from scholarships and other study grants;

(d) Equal opportunities for access to programs of continuing education, including adult literacy programs;

(e) Access to educational information to help in insuring the health and well-being of families.

Article 10

1. All appropriate measures shall be taken to insure to women, equal rights with men in the field of economic and social life, and in particular:

(a) The right without discrimination on grounds of marital status or any other grounds, to receive vocational training, to work, to free choice of profession and employment, and to professional and vocational advancement;

(b) The right to equal remuneration with men and to equality of treatment in respect of work of equal value;

(c) The right to leave with pay, retirement privileges and provision for security in respect of unemployment, sickness, old age or other incapacity to work;

(d) The right to receive family allowances on equal terms with men.

2. In order to prevent discrimination against women on account of marriage or maternity and to insure their effective right to work, measures shall be taken to prevent their dismissal in the event of marriage or maternity and to provide paid maternity leave, with the guarantee of returning to former employment, and to provide the necessary social services, including child-care facilities.

3. Measures taken to protect women in certain types of work, for reasons inherent in their physical nature, shall not be regarded as discriminatory.

Article 11

The principle of equality of rights of men and women demands implementation in all states in accordance with the principles of the United Nations Charter and of the Universal Declaration of Human Rights.

Governments, nongovernmental organizations and individuals are urged therefore to do all in their power to promote the implementation of the principles contained in this Declaration.

STILL INEQUALITIES IN SOCIALIST SOCIETY [2]

Even in a socialist society where equal opportunity for women is part of public policy it is still difficult for them to rise to positions of power and influence in anything like the same numbers as men. Although many more women work in the German Democratic Republic proportionately than in the Federal Republic, Germany's other "half," the pattern of employment in the senior levels is remarkably similar.

This is one of the conclusions from a PEP (Political and Economic Planning) study of women's careers in the two Germanies, which is the latest part of a three-year Leverhulme Trust research project. Research into facts and policies on women's careers in both socialist and capitalist societies has been the subject of attention by this team from 1966 to 1969. The two Germanies provide a particularly important and interesting pair of cases because at the time of their partition in 1945 German national culture was at its most homogeneous, under National Socialist rule.

Since the division of the country into two, very different policies have been pursued by their governments. As far as the careers of women are concerned the difference lies in the avowed policy of sex equality in eastern Germany, the GDR, as against the much more traditional attitudes in the western half, Federal Germany, which, though modified, still preserve the view that woman's place is in the home.

Both countries have a surplus of women over men; 113 women to 100 men in the Federal Republic, 119 women to 100 men in the GDR. In his introduction, Michael Fogarty comments that this surplus, and general postwar emergency,

[2] From the *Christian Science Monitor*. p 10. Mr. 22, '71 Reprinted by permission from *The Christian Science Monitor*. © 1971 The Christian Science Publishing Society. All rights reserved.

may explain why so many women work in western Germany, although the official line is contrary to such a development. It is possible that in time tradition may reassert itself. The eastern German female surplus, like the western, is the product of war casualties among men, but in the east it has been aggravated by emigration to the west of single men.

The proportion of women who work in East Germany is far higher than in West Germany, with more married women having jobs. The state has attempted to deal with the problem of "overload" in the family where both parents work by providing nursery schools and home help services, and there are arrangements for the hire of domestic appliances. Nevertheless, it is still the women who do the housework in East Germany, and it has been calculated that as a result men have ten hours more free time a week than women.

In the west the problem of "overload" has been partially solved in the customary market economy style—the supply of relatively inexpensive domestic appliances by private enterprise. At the same time, in the west women still tend to regard their main role in life as wives and mothers, to the extent that even when they do reach university (they form 29 percent of the student population) their "dropout" rate is nearly twice that of men. There is a negative attitude both to women students and to their appointment to academic posts, especially very senior appointments.

As most senior appointments in West Germany require an academic qualification, the Abitur, it follows that a majority of women do not attain the minimal qualification for a career leading to a "top job." Women tend to occupy the middle and junior grades in most professions, and remarkably few reach the level of administrator in central government, judge, professor, or head teacher. There is a strong objection to appointing women to managerial posts, so that in business where a woman is at the head of a firm it will be a small one and probably inherited from her husband.

One result of the tendency for middle-class West German women to continue working after marriage, as increasing numbers are doing especially in teaching, is for the gap between the lower and higher income groups to widen. Marriages are generally within class boundaries. Working-class women have less opportunity to earn their family a second income. In future, therefore, income differentials between social classes will increase, but the general obstacles to women's advancement look to be remaining.

The same barriers, traditional attitudes, and habits of mind on the part of both men and women, have affected women's careers in East Germany as well. In spite of the fact that the GDR has the highest proportion of working women in Europe, and that the education and employment systems may be said to be biased in favor of women, only 1 graduate woman in 19 reaches a senior post in the party or in government or industry compared with a ratio of 1 in 3 for male graduates.

As in West Germany, also, an examination of rates of pay shows that in East Germany women are not paid the rate to which their qualifications entitle them, while men are often paid above this rate.

There are more women students in the East than in the West, 1 in 322 as against 1 in 452, but here again they gravitate to the service professions, education, and health, assuming the role traditionally allotted to the working woman in western countries—that of taking on "womanly" occupations such as nursing, infant teaching, welfare and social work.

Thus the results of what may be regarded as a national-scale "controlled experiment" to see how the place of women in society can be affected by a difference of philosophy and regime shows fairly conclusively that in both kinds of society men still predominate in the powerful and influential upper levels.

WHERE DID IT ALL GO WRONG? [3]

Look at the index of any cultural history: ancient Greece, medieval Europe, Renaissance Italy, postwar America. There, after pages of the familiar headings under which we classify the phenomena of human experience—art and architecture, games and pastimes, medicine, politics, trade, war, etc.—the reader will almost always come upon the entry "Women," in nearly every case followed by some such phrase as "position of." What won't be found is the entry "Men, position of," for the very good reason that the history of men has been synonymous in the minds of nearly all historians with the history of civilization itself.

Such a circumstance is more revealing than an avalanche of statistics about unequal social or economic opportunities or a thousand and one tales of particular cruelties or injustices. Similarly, the nature of most languages tells us more about the hierarchical structure of male-female relationships than all the physical horror stories that could be compiled. Mistreatment of women by men may, theoretically, be a matter of individual if widespread delinquency, a series of failures to live up to an ostensibly universal moral code, a series of blows without ideology; besides, it has been argued, men also suffer from the depredations and exploitations of more powerful males. But that our language employs the words "man" and "mankind" as terms for the whole human race demonstrates that male dominance, the *idea* of masculine superiority, is perennial, institutional and rooted at the deepest levels of our historical experience.

Whether or not it is unjust is another question. And whether or not, if it is unjust, it can be overthrown is still another. There are some injustices that seem ordained by nature, and this is the heart of the problem. The organization of sexual relations along the broad lines of masculine activity, strength, genius and rule and feminine passivity, weakness, mental inferiority and subjecthood is so firmly

[3] Article by Richard Gilman, social and literary critic. *Life*. 71:48-55. Ag. 13, '71. © 1971 Time Inc.

established in consciousness that even to contemplate any radical change is deeply disturbing. John Stuart Mill, one of the rare great male defenders of women's case against men, wrote a hundred years ago that "everything which is usual appears natural," so that "the subjection of women to men being a universal custom, any departure from it quite naturally appears unnatural." This conviction of the fundamental "naturalness" of the ways that power, authority and human definitions are distributed between men and women is without doubt the central cause of the violent anxiety with which, under the mask of amusement, irritation or scorn, most men, and most women as well, have reacted to the recent wave of feminism.

What is the history of this custom which seems always to have been regarded as a decision of nature? To begin with, as the anthropologist Claude Lévi-Strauss has flatly stated, "public or simply social authority always belongs to men." The myth of earlier societies of dominant women, Amazons or mother-rulers, has a long standing. But it remains a myth; all that anthropology has been able to conclude is that matriarchies have indeed existed, but this doesn't mean that women were dominant in such societies, only that descent and inheritance were figured from the mother, an outcome, presumably, of early man's ignorance of his own role in procreation.

From the beginning of recorded history, patriarchy is everywhere established. The Jewish tradition, for example, was heavily masculine. The Old Testament devotes inordinate space to the listing of long lines of male descent to the point where it would seem that for centuries women "begat" nothing but male offspring. Although there are heroines in the Old Testament—Judith, Esther and the like—it's clear that they functioned like the heroines of Greek drama and later of French: as counterweights in the imaginations of certain sensitive men to the degraded position of women in actual life. The true spirit of the tradition was unabashedly revealed in the prayer men recited every day in the synagogue: "Blessed art Thou, O Lord . . . for not making me a woman."

Greek civilization was also thoroughly male. The so-called masculine virtues of strength, daring and prowess were the ones celebrated: male homosexual love was widely considered a higher mode than heterosexual. Women had almost no legal rights and, although (as throughout history) individual women might obtain moral or psychic power over individual men, women as a whole played no part in public life or rule. Hesiod [Greek poet] called women a necessary evil and related the myth of Pandora, which holds her responsible for the ills of the world. More significantly for the future, some Greek philosophers constructed a radical view of women either as metaphysically evil or as deficient. Pythagoras wrote that "there is a good principle which has created order, light and man; and a bad principle which has created chaos, darkness and woman." Aristotle described women as "female by virtue of a certain incapacity. . . . [They] are weaker and cooler by nature than . . . males and we must regard the female character as a kind of natural defectiveness."

During the Roman era some women played larger public roles than they had in Greece. Yet such authority as a woman might attain was very often the result of her connection with a man; the wives, mothers and mistresses of emperors, for instance, exerted influence by means of reflected or symbolic power. Legal rights were slowly acquired, but in the second century B.C., Cato the Censor could still tell Roman men: "If you catch your wife in adultery, you would kill her with impunity, without a trial; but if she were to catch you, she would not dare lay a finger on you, and indeed she has no right."

With the emergence of Christianity, the full complex history of women's position in Western society began. At first glance, Christianity appears to have significantly raised the status of women. The church enforced monogamy (whose absence had benefited only men), stressed a single moral standard for both sexes and was the first institution to defend women's right to inherit property. In the Middle Ages monastic orders for women offered girls their only alternative to marriages that were often loveless and sometimes tyrannical. Most broadly, St. Paul's assertion that "there is neither Jew nor Greek . . . slave nor free . . . male nor female . . . for you are all one in Christ Jesus" enunciated a principle of equality between the sexes such as had never formally been present in human society.

But there was another strain in Christianity that weighed against its spiritual egalitarianism, and that was, of course, its mistrust of the physical, its perception of the world as balanced between soul and matter, with the latter an eternal danger. The church's deep suspicion of the body, of sexual being and, hence, of women—submerged so much more completely than men in the reproductive cycle—profoundly affected its thinking and practice. In doctrine women may have been spiritually equal, but in the minds of almost all churchmen they were dangerous, unfathomable, potentials for damnation.

On the questions of sex and marriage, the Church Fathers had great difficulty reconciling the biblical command "be fruitful and multiply" with their insistence on the transcendent beauty and virtue of virginity. St. Paul's dictum that "it is better to marry than to burn" became the reluctant church position. St. Ambrose probably expressed the prevailing monastic view when he wrote, in a particularly flagrant example of sophistry, that marriages were after all acceptable, for otherwise how could virgins be born? Sex outside marriage or within it for pleasure alone was, of course, proscribed.

St. Ambrose, who was one of the milder priestly misogynists, also wrote that "Adam was deceived by Eve, not Eve by Adam . . . it is right that he whom that woman induced to sin should assume the role of guide lest he fall again through feminine instability." This notion of a guilt attaching to woman beyond that for original sin, which she naturally shared with man, runs through much early church writing.

The biblical story, like many creation myths, is permeated with a sense of male priority and a corresponding sense of the female as auxiliary, a secondary being. That God himself is conceived of as male is of course the ultimate expression of such sentiments.

It has been argued that the cult of the Virgin, which was flourishing by the twelfth century, was evidence of a countermovement in the church to the denigration of women. The Virgin was indeed raised to semidivine status; cathedrals were erected in her honor, and even in the game of chess, the piece called the minister became the virgin queen, with unlimited powers. Yet the same religious men who sang Mary's praises continued to fulminate against women in general. St. Thomas, writing at the height of the Virgin cult, called woman "defective and accidental . . . male gone awry," and added, with the bizarre imposture of science that has plagued men's thinking about women through the centuries, that she is probably "the result of some weakness in the [father's] generative power . . . or of some external factor, like the south wind, which is damp." It seems clear that the Virgin was celebrated as an abstract, *sinless* woman, one without sexual being, in effect the anti-Eve. The split which arose from this—madonna and whore—has persisted to our own time.

Still, by all accounts the religious horror of woman's sexual nature had little restraint on actual morals during most of the Middle Ages. The facades of many cathedrals might depict woman in sculpture as the incarnation of the Vice of Unchastity and show her writhing in hell, but the average man was doubtless quite willing to risk his immortal soul for sexual pleasures. Not until the translation of the Bible into the vernacular and the corresponding advent of Protestantism and the rise of the Puritan ethic was the ordinary consciousness much affected by warnings against woman as temptress. Even so, when in 1558 John Knox

[Scottish reformer], outraged at England's having a Catholic queen, wrote his *First Blast of the Trumpet Against the Monstrous Regiment of Women*, he stressed woman's presumption, foolishness and instability rather than her erotic dangers. The ordinary consciousness, both male and female, remained convinced that women were inferior and ought to be subordinate to men.

As the Middle Ages gave way to bourgeois society and later to the industrial era, such old severities were slowly mitigated. Purely physical oppression was widely replaced, at least among the middle and upper classes, by much more subtle forms of dominance. Yet well into the nineteenth century, there were reports of women being sold by their husbands "for a quart of beer or an ounce of thick twist."

As the modern age took shape, women gained more and more legal rights, such as the right to own and dispose of property or to sue for divorce, yet they fell increasingly into a condition Mill called "bribery and intimidation combined." One significant aspect of eighteenth and nineteenth century social reality was the flourishing of the woman of leisure, the coddled wife or daughter whom Thorstein Veblen [American social scientist, author of *The Theory of the Leisure Class*, 1899] described as "useless and expensive, and . . . consequently valuable as evidence of [the] pecuniary strength" of her husband or father. Another development was the growth of a patronizing or sentimental consideration of the female. Lord Chesterfield's letters speak of women as "only children of a larger growth; they have an entertaining tattle. . . . A man of sense only trifles with them, plays with them, humours and flatters them." And Keats cries out apropos of a girl of his imagination: "God! She is like a milk-white lamb that bleats/for man's protection."

This demeaning protectiveness was related to a view of women as *morally* superior to men, "nobler" by virtue of their delicacy and self-sacrificing nature, as demonstrated in their maternal roles. Such masculine sentiment bristled with hypocrisy. It was useful to men that domestic and nurturing functions be filled by women, but when the latter made gestures toward larger interests and responsibilities, they were suppressed. The "petticoat reformers" of Manchester in the early nineteenth century, women who agitated publicly against inhuman conditions in the mills, were described by a leading newspaper as "degraded females" who had deserted "their station" and shed the "sacred characters" of wife and mother. Later, Victorian England witnessed rampant prostitution and a huge traffic in pornography behind a facade of domestic propriety and a reigning ideal of "womanhood."

The nineteenth century also saw a new and virulent outbreak of misogyny. Literary and philosophical rather than religious, it can be found in the writings of some of the era's greatest minds. Philosophers like Schopenhauer and Nietzsche constructed elaborate portraits of women's inferiority. To Schopenhauer they were "childish, frivolous and shortsighted" and existed "solely for the propagation of the species"; Nietzsche inveighed against their "pedantry, superficiality . . . presumption, petty licentiousness and immodesty" and thought that a man who believed they were equal to himself was a "shallow" man. More pseudoscientifically, Charles Darwin found women constitutionally inferior to men in anything "requiring deep thought, reason or imagination, or merely the use of the senses or hands," which would appear to say it all.

But the misogyny with the most far-reaching implications was that of Sigmund Freud. An archetypal Victorian sentimentalist who wrote that women's destiny was "determined through beauty, charm and sweetness" and who dealt with his own wife as a patron treats a dependent, Freud at the same time enunciated a scientific schema of feminine sexual and intellectual being that powerfully reinforced age-old prejudices. In the tradition of Aristotle and St. Thomas, he considered woman an insufficient or defective creature whose entire psychosexual life was shaped by her having been "deprived" of a penis, and whose moral and social existence was marked by "envy," "insincerity," "secretiveness," an underdeveloped sense of justice and honor and an incapacity for the "higher human tasks."

So deep-seated was Freud's "scientifically" based misogyny that he was led to declare that "nature has paid less careful attention to the demands of the female functions than to those of masculinity" and to identify a "repudiation of femininity" in biology itself. Yet such explicit expressions of bias were less significant than his pervasive and absolute conviction of male primacy and centrality in human affairs.

Freud's ideas about women, institutionalized now in many species of psychoanalysis and, in debased form, in popular consciousness, pose more centrally than those of any other modern thinker the chief questions about the relationship of the sexes. What is just beginning to be recognized is that throughout his inquiry into human sexuality, otherwise so productive of liberating insights and discoveries, Freud unconsciously employed a masculine model for both sexes; on this basis women could scarcely fail to appear aberrant and "abnormal." What is also being recognized is how startlingly his "contemporary" ideas mirror the oldest historical elements of antifeminine feeling, and thus how profoundly rooted must be the biases and irrationalities which surround the female in the minds of men.

In his important study *Sex and Repression in Savage Society,* anthropologist Bronislaw Malinowski wrote that "education consists in the last instance in the building up of complex and artificial habit responses, of the organization of emotions into sentiments." Nothing could be more instructive about the history of men's treatment of women. For women's "inferiority" is almost entirely the product of education, which for almost all of history has been in men's hands. (Not until well into the nineteenth century were women even allowed to attend college in England and America.) Through education, formal and informal, and by direct teaching or assimilation from the atmosphere, what begin as emotions in men become fixed as sentiments, more or less vague ideas suffused with feeling, which purport to announce what women are like and, more grandiosely, what they eternally *are*.

That they are physically inferior (the author of a Renaissance treatise on painting wrote: "I will make you acquainted with the proportions of a man; I omit those of a woman, because there is not one of them perfectly proportioned"); that they are intellectually lesser; that they represent disorder; that they are frivolous, inconstant and untrustworthy; that, finally, they are chiefly or solely fitted to be wives, mistresses and mothers—all this is, as we have seen, what men have thought and felt, but it is also an elaborate set of rationalizations. These sentiments have come to serve as justifications for men's preeminence in the sexual, economic, political and social spheres.

The origins of men's ascendancy in these realms undoubtedly lay in their relatively greater size and physical strength and in the fact that women were burdened and made less mobile by pregnancy and maternity. As social development went on, the stronger males came to impose distinctions between their "nobler" functions and, as Veblen said, "the uneventful diligence of women," and constructed a hierarchy of human valuation with themselves at the top.

This moral superiority based on an original physical one is the reason why, in an age of technology, when physical prowess is less and less decisive and when the reproductive processes are increasingly less limiting and debilitating to women, most men continue to maintain their theories of women's disqualification from the "important" business of the world and to defend their universe of authority against those "aggressive," "envious," "unwomanly" women who want to have an equal share in it. It is also a reason for the curious fact that in the prevailing masculine ethos, big women, athletic and muscular women, are regarded as aberrations. The conclusion is inescapable that men *want* women to be weak, dependent, inadequate in crucial ways.

One theory about this is the narrowly economic one: that women have been kept weak in order that the more powerful "class" of men may simply and directly exploit them—which Engels first articulated a century ago and which some Marxist feminists uphold now. But this surely makes too practical and conscious a matter out of something that is deeply psychological and metaphysical: a mode of emotional response, an attitude toward existence, a way of organizing human relations so as to justify roles and behavior. While men's supremacy may have suited their economic aims, it also supported their moral and psychological ones. Virginia Woolf was closer to the truth than the Marxists when she observed that "women have served all these centuries as looking glasses possessing the magic and delicious power of reflecting the figure of man at twice its natural size."

Yet even this is not the whole story. Men may have sought a magnification of their egos through a contrast with women, whom they have therefore kept diminished, but they have also sought in the female an explanation for their own existential unease, a scapegoat for their own guilty pride and a figure on whom to place the burden of their own internal division. Simone de Beauvoir writes of "that mysterious . . . reality known as feminity." This "reality," which women have had to carry about and suffer under, is a masculine invention: it has been male minds which, with what strikes us as the most astonishing arrogance when we are free to see it, have determined the nature of feminity, at the same time making certain that they defined masculinity as well.

In *The Canterbury Tales*, Chaucer has the Wyfe of Bath comment on the immemorial silence of women in the face of men's continual discussion of them: "By God, if wommen hadde writen stories/As clerkes han with-inne hir oratories,/ They wolde han writen of men more wikkednesse/Than all the Mark of Adam may redresse!"

Until very recently, women have not usually felt free enough to write about men, or about themselves for that matter: "Women should keep silence in church," St. Paul said, and for centuries all but a handful kept silence in the world as well. In the vacuum this left, men inserted their various myths, legends and imaginary portraits of the feminine: the woman as gorgon, harpy, siren, earth mother, sphinx, muse and witch. The common element in all these masks, which there have always been women happy enough to wear, is the notion or intuition of the female as uncanny, a creature from another world, the incarnation of "otherness."

This mysteriousness of women to men centers on the female's far greater intimacy with nature by virtue of being so much more fully involved in the most fundamental biological processes. Women have, in fact, always represented uncontrolled nature to men. The myth of women's sexual insatiability is testimony to something feared, a destruction by passionate ordeal or, at best, a challenge one cannot meet.

Everything having to do with women's reproductive functions has troubled men, whose myth making has been encouraged by centuries of ignorance. One theory of Greek medicine was that male fetuses were completely formed in thirty days, while females took forty-two, the males being superior because of their quicker "ripening." Aristotle believed that male chicks developed from ovoid eggs—the ones closest to the perfection of "eggness"—but in the Middle Ages, Albertus Magnus [German scholastic philosopher] insisted that males came from spheroid eggs, since the sphere is the perfect geometric figure. In many cultures boy babies were believed to develop in the right side of the womb, girls in the left, the "sinister" or evil side. The female ovum wasn't actually discovered until 1827, and the cyclical relationship between menstruation and ovulation wasn't clearly established until the turn of the century. Menstruation has been the subject of universal taboos, and birth itself has been felt to be unclean. Obviously, not all men have felt these things and fewer feel them consciously now. But they have characterized the general male response and, like a great many other elements of man's relationship to woman,

they live on in the unconscious and determine actual behavior. In the same way that a majority of men would
doubtless deny that they feel superior to women, they would
deny that they are troubled by women's sexuality, except as
a matter of their own desire and its complications, but the
disturbance continues to show itself in the way society is
organized.

Yet the uneasiness—even dread—which men have felt in
the face of women goes beyond the narrowly sexual to touch
their deepest sense of self. The human struggle against nature is essentially a masculine activity. Throughout history,
mankind has attempted to rise above nature or bend it to
man's will. Women have been far less easily seduced than
men into the battle against nature, precisely because of their
greater immersion in the procreative process. In a strange
defect of sympathy, men have attempted to keep women in
their narrow roles as sexual objects and perpetuators of the
species, and at the same time despised them for it.

Laws, art, science, commerce, religion, sport, moral systems, political structures: everything we think of as civilization has been very largely the creation of men, not because
women have been unable to contribute to it but because
they have been prevented from doing so. "All the geniuses
who are born women are lost to the public good," Stendhal
wrote 150 years ago. From the Bible to Freud, woman's
"nature" has been adduced as the reason for her failure to
be part of the making of the human world of institutions
and values. One of the great ironies of human history is that
men have feared women as the carnal force opposed to culture and simultaneously denied the education, wherewithal
and morale necessary for them to participate in it.

The strictures have undeniably become less and less
physical and legal. For several centuries, women have been
kept in their "place" by a more or less informal structure of
belief and sentiment, a determination of what they are supposed to be and do which operates independently of facts.
The great majority of women, educated to no other possi-

bility, pressed and pushed and cajoled from infancy toward the narrow ends of marriage and family and intimidated like any subject class, have accepted men's definitions and obeyed the seemingly natural order of things. If nothing else, Women's Liberationists are challenging for the first time on a large scale these definitions of female nature and duty.

In doing it, some of them have alienated potential sympathizers by presenting themselves as fanatics whose ideas and proposals (the abolition of the family, the beauty of lesbianism) have outraged traditional sensibility. Perhaps the most frequent charge against Women's Liberation is that its adherents want to be like men, an accusation which, whether made by a man or a woman, is another indication of male supremacy. That they might wish to be like *themselves*, to be what they decide to be, to determine their own reality free of the imposed definitions of others seems a difficult notion for those who have already decided on the fixed nature of the world and the people in it.

No woman, and naturally no man either, rose to attack Rousseau two hundred years ago when he placed in *Emile,* his blueprint for an ideal education, this sketch of female existence:

the whole education of women should be relative to men. To please them, to be useful to them, to win their love and esteem, to bring them up when young, to tend them when grown, to advise and console them, and to make life sweet and pleasant to them; these are the duties of women at all times, and what they ought to learn from infancy.

By and large, they are still being taught this. Not long ago Dr. Spock wrote in a magazine directed toward young women: "Biologically and temperamentally, I believe, women were made to be concerned first and foremost with child care, husband care and home care. . . ." [In a letter to the editor of *Life,* published in the October 2, 1971, issue, Dr. Spock pointed out that his quoted sentence read in full: ". . . though of course they also are capable of taking on most of the other occupations and interests that have been men's challenges."—Ed.]

In the mid-nineteenth century, when feminism began to be a force for the first time, John Stuart Mill's wife, Harriet, composed a majestic and unanswerable reply to the arrogance of men like Rousseau and Spock. "We deny the right," she wrote, "of any portion of the species to decide for another portion, or any individual for another individual, what is and what is not their 'proper sphere.' The proper sphere for all human beings is the largest and highest which they are able to attain to."

A DECADE OF WIDENING HORIZONS [4]

After a decade of striking change, the American woman is now considerably more likely to attend college, work, live alone, marry late, be divorced or separated, and outlive her husband than she was at the start of the 1960s.

These are among the findings of an assessment of the status of women, based on new data from the 1970 census, Government surveys and reports, and interviews with Census Bureau analysts.

Some of the changes continue trends dating back four and five decades. Others suggest new trends. Taken together, said George Hay Brown, director of the Census Bureau, "These are social changes of the first magnitude. Women in the seventies are rapidly moving toward full equality."

The changes in employment and education among women are among the most dramatic.

Of the 13.8 million new jobs that developed in the sixties, women took 8.4 million, nearly two thirds. As a result, by 1970, more than 43 percent of all adult women were in the labor force. This represented the quickening of a trend dating to 1920. The figure was 37 percent in 1960, 34 percent in 1950 and 23 percent in 1920.

The proportion of married women in the work force rose even faster, from a quarter to a third in the sixties. This is largely accounted for by soaring numbers of women thirty-five to forty-five years old who return to work after their children start growing up. Still faster gains were recorded in education. The number of white women with at least four years of high school climbed from 65 percent to 80 [percent]. Among black women, the figure went from 40 percent to 61 [percent]. And women with some college education rose 160 percent, against 100 percent for men.

Other aspects of significant change include the following:

The ratio of men to women dropped to its lowest point in the century. There are now 104 million women and fewer than 99 million men—94.8 men for every 100 women. . . .

These changes are explained by a lengthening of the longevity gap. According to the most recent figures, census analysts say, women live about seven years longer than men. . . .

The proportion of adult women living alone or with unrelated roommates rose 50 percent, to 7.6 million, about a tenth of all adult women. Women over sixty-five, some four million of whom now live independently, accounted for most of the increase. But women twenty to thirty-four years old in this category increased at the fastest rate, rising 109 percent, to 800,000.

Some of the increase in employment and independent residence is accounted for by a rise in the proportion of women who are divorced or separated. In 1960, both categories totaled about 7 percent of all married women. In 1970, the figure approached 10 percent. This increase demonstrates that "a woman now can maintain herself without the need to remarry," said Conrad F. Taeuber, associate director of the Census Bureau.

About 95 percent of all women still eventually marry, but at a later age. After remaining stable for twenty years, the median age at marriage climbed half a year in the sixties to 20.8 years for women and 23.2 for men.

Explaining the Changes

Analysts offer a host of explanations for such changes. In the employment area, they cite the high demand for labor in the sixties and the changing nature of the structure of occupations.

"The percentage of heavy muscle-jobs—farmers, steel puddlers—is going down. We are moving from a muscle economy to a machine/service economy," said Mr. Brown, the census director. "Opportunities are increasing."

This increase, analysts believe, has coincided with two other factors—an increase in the number of low-income wives who work because of a need for money, and an increase in the number of wives at all income levels who work because of a need for satisfaction.

Census experts cite changes among women at high income levels as strongly suggestive of the latter factor, since such women are much less likely to work because of economic need.

For example, in 1960, among the wives of professional men, only 30 percent worked. By 1970, the figure had risen to 41 percent.

What we see here is probably true also among many lower-income women as well, but we can't document it [said Daniel B. Levine, director of census surveys]. They may spend much of what they earn on day care, lunch and getting to work. But it's worth it to them, to be able to get out of the house and have contact with adults.

Another employment factor cited by experts is the increased availability of child-care and labor-saving products, like convenience foods and a wide variety of home appliances, which help loosen the wife's apron strings.

"The point is a bit circular," Mr. Taeuber said. "You can argue that, because many women now work, they create a market for these products and services. But you can also argue that, because they are available, more women find it possible to work. It is likely that both arguments are right."

The kinds of jobs taken by women have changed significantly. Three of every four clerical workers are now women, against one out of two in 1940. Women now make up 61 percent of all service workers, against 39 percent in 1940.

The proportion of professional and technical workers who are women has declined slightly, however, in the same period, from 42 percent to 40.

As of 1969, women earned less than men working in the same occupational categories, ranging from 48 percent of the male average salary in sales to 72 percent in teaching.

But analysts say most statistical evidence does not validly demonstrate discrimination against women.

Elizabeth Waldman, a Department of Labor authority, said, "They may have to put convenience of location or flexibility of hours above earnings. Married women may not be in a position to accept jobs with overtime pay or to accept a promotion to a job with heavier responsibilities."

IV. BIOLOGY AND THE SOCIAL ROLE

EDITOR'S INTRODUCTION

No aspect of the debate over woman's role generates such vehement controversy as the arguments over biology, culture, and function in society. Why are women generally more passive than men? Why have there been so few women geniuses? Is the cause an innate characteristic of female biology, or does cultural conditioning from infancy hammer women into a special mold?

Evidence can be summoned to support several sides of these questions. The findings are still inconclusive. These issues, however, are at the heart of any serious discussion of women and society.

The first three articles in this final section explore the broad issues of biological abilities and cultural conditioning. Jo Freeman, a feminist writer and scholar, demonstrates that girls are rigorously trained from infancy to be unaggressive, passive, and docile. Opening with a quotation from the noted French author Simone de Beauvoir to the effect that passivity is imposed by teachers and society, she presents a comprehensive survey of sociological and psychological studies showing that conditioning causes women to behave as they do.

In the following article Tom Alexander, an associate editor of *Fortune*, explores current research indicating definite differences in specific mental abilities of boys and girls. Boys, for example, excel in mechanical aptitudes and certain kinds of spatial reasoning, whereas girls consistently excel in verbal skills. After these two rather technical articles, there is a more general commentary by the noted pediatrician Dr. Benjamin Spock, who holds that boys and girls do differ in behavior right from the start.

Next, critic Diana Trilling comments on the effects of a predominantly male culture on female upbringing. She predicts a diminishing of society's admiration for the ruggedly "masculine" man or the helpless "feminine" woman.

From these more general assessments of women and society, we turn to the two specific roles that offer the greatest obstacles to some of the feminists' goals: women as wives and mothers. A prime goal of the movement is twenty-four-hour day care for children, thus freeing women to work when they choose. Here the more radical clash sharply with those who believe that at least in early childhood a one-to-one relationship with a mother is vitally important to normal child development. Three articles explore these issues: first, a survey of working mothers and their demand for child care facilities; second, an article from *Woman's Day*, discussing the importance of alert mothering to a child's preschool development; third, an opinion by Dr. Spock on the role of both mother and father in child rearing.

Through many of the discussions of Women's Liberation there runs a serious challenge to traditional marriage and family structure. Some Women's Liberationists reject marriage outright. If a mother is at work and the child in a public nursery, what will become of the family as a viable social unit? Morton Hunt, an author who has done frequent studies of marriage and family structure, surveys the many challenges to traditional marriage—Women's Liberation, communal living, group marriage, divorce—and concludes that marriage as an institution will survive. What he does see, however, is a continuing trend away from what is termed the old "patriarchal monogamy" pattern toward a more "companionate marriage" of equals.

One of the feminists' most articulate and concerned advocates, Gloria Steinem, concludes the book with a scenario of what she thinks it would be like if women achieved all that some are asking for them. It would be, she believes, a far more humane and less competitive world.

THE SOCIAL CONSTRUCTION OF THE
SECOND SEX [1]

The passivity that is the essential characteristic of the "feminine" woman is a trait that develops in her from the earliest years. But it is wrong to assert a biological datum is concerned; it is in fact a destiny imposed upon her by her teachers and by society.—Simone de Beauvoir

During the last thirty years social science has paid scant attention to women, confining its explorations of humanity to the male. Research has generally reinforced the sex stereotypes of popular mythology that women are essentially nurturant/expressive/passive and men instrumental/active/aggressive. Social scientists have tended to justify these stereotypes rather than analyze their origins, their value, or their effect.

In part this is due to the general conservatism and reluctance to question the status quo which has characterized the social sciences during this era of the feminine mystique. In part it is attributable to what Alice S. Rossi describes as the "pervasive permeation of psychoanalytic thinking throughout American society." The result has been a social science which is more a mechanism of social control than of social inquiry. Rather than trying to analyze why, it has only described what. Rather than exploring how men and women came to be the way they are, it has taken their condition as an irremediable given and sought to justify it on the basis of "biological" differences.

Nonetheless, the assumption that psychology recapitulates physiology has begun to crack. Masters and Johnson shattered the myth of woman's natural sexual passivity—on which her psychological passivity was claimed to rest. Research is just beginning into the other areas. Even without this new research new interpretations of the old data are

[1] Essay by Jo Freeman. In *Roles Women Play: Readings Toward Women's Liberation*, ed. by M. H. Garskof. Brooks/Cole. '71. p 123-41. The author of this essay is a graduate student in political science at the University of Chicago and the editor of a forthcoming anthology on women from a feminist perspective. © 1970 by Jo Freeman. All rights reserved. Reprinted by permission.

being explored. What these new interpretations say is that women are the way they are because they've been trained to be that way. As Sandra and Daryl Bem put it: "We overlook the fact that the society that has spent twenty years carefully marking the woman's ballot for her has nothing to lose in that twenty-first year by pretending to let her cast it for the alternative of her choice. Society has controlled not her alternatives, but her motivation to choose any but the one of those alternatives."

This motivation is controlled through the socialization process. Women are raised to want to fill the social roles in which society needs them. They are trained to model themselves after the accepted image and to meet as individuals the expectations that are held for women as a group. Therefore, to understand how most women are socialized we must first understand how they see themselves and are seen by others. Several studies have been done on this. Quoting from one of them, David McClelland stated that "the female image is characterized as small, weak, soft and light. In the United States it is also dull, peaceful, relaxed, cold, rounded, passive and slow." A more thorough study by E. M. Bennett and L. R. Cohen which asked men and women to choose out of a long list of adjectives those which most closely applied to themselves showed that women strongly felt themselves to be uncertain, anxious, nervous, hasty, careless, fearful, dull, childish, helpless, sorry, timid, clumsy, stupid, silly, and domestic. On a more positive side, women felt that they were understanding, tender, sympathetic, pure, generous, affectionate, loving, moral, kind, grateful, and patient.

This is not a very favorable self-image but it does correspond fairly well with the social myths about what women are like. The image has some nice qualities, but they are not the ones normally required for that kind of achievement to which society gives its highest social rewards. Now one can justifiably question both the idea of achievement and the qualities necessary for it, but this is not the place to do so.

Rather, ᵔcause the current standards are the ones which
women have been told they do not meet, the purpose here
will be to look at the socialization process as a mechanism
to keep them from doing so. We will also need to analyze
some of the social expectations about women and about
what is defined as a successful *woman* (not a successful
person) because this is inextricably bound up with the
socialization process. All people are socialized to meet the
social expectations held for them, and it is only when this
process fails to do so (as is currently happening on several
fronts) that it is at all questioned.

Let us first examine the effects on women of minority-
group status. Here, an interesting parallel emerges, but it is
one fraught with much heresy. When we look at the *results*
of female socialization we find a strong similarity between
what our society labels, even extols, as the typical "feminine"
character structure and that of oppressed peoples in this
country and elsewhere.

In his classic study on *The Nature of Prejudice*, Allport
devotes a chapter to "Traits Due to Victimization." Included
are such personality characteristics as sensitivity, submission,
fantasies of power, desire for protection, indirectness, ingratiation, petty revenge and sabotage, sympathy, extremes of
both self- and group-hatred and self- and group-glorification,
display of flashy status symbols, compassion for the underprivileged, identification with the dominant group's norms,
and passivity. Allport was primarily concerned with Jews
and Negroes, but compare his characterization with the very
thorough review of the literature on sex differences among
young children made by Lewis Terman and Leona Tyler.
For girls, they listed such traits as sensitivity, conformity to
social pressures, response to environment, ease of social control, ingratiation, sympathy, low levels of aspiration, compassion for the underprivileged, and anxiety. They found
that girls compared to boys were more nervous, unstable,
neurotic, socially dependent, submissive, had less self-confi-

dence, lower opinions of themselves and of girls in general, and were more timid, emotional, ministrative, fearful, and passive.

Girls' perceptions of themselves were also distorted. Stevenson Smith found that although girls make consistently better school grades than boys until late high school, their opinion of themselves grows progressively worse with age and their opinion of boys and boys' abilities grows better. Boys, however, have an increasingly better opinion of themselves and worse opinion of girls as they grow older.

These distortions become so gross that, according to Philip Goldberg, reporting in *Trans-Action,* by the time girls reach college they have become prejudiced against women. He gave college girls sets of booklets containing six identical professional articles in traditional male, female, and neutral fields. The articles were identical, but the names of the authors were not. For example, an article in one set would bear the name John T. McKay and in another set the same article would be authored by Joan T. McKay. Each booklet contained three articles by "women" and three by "men." Questions at the end of each article asked the students to rate the articles on value, persuasiveness and profundity and the authors on writing style and competence. The male authors fared better in every field, even such "feminine" areas as art history and dietetics. Goldberg concluded that "women are prejudiced against female professionals and, regardless of the actual accomplishments of these professionals, will firmly refuse to recognize them as the equals of their male colleagues."

This combination of group self-hate and distortion of perceptions to justify that group self-hate are precisely the traits typical of a "minority-group character structure." It has been noted time and time again. Kenneth and Mamie Clark's finding of this pattern in Negro children in segregated schools contributed to the 1954 Supreme Court decision that outlawed such schools. These traits, as well as the others typical of the "feminine" stereotype, have been found in the

Indians under British rule, in the Algerians under the French, and in black Americans. There seems to be a correlation between being "feminine" and experiencing status deprivation.

This pattern repeats itself even within cultures. In giving TATs [Thematic Apperception Tests] to women in Japanese villages, George De Vos discovered that those from fishing villages where the status position of women was higher than in farming communities were more assertive, not as guilt-ridden and were more willing to ignore the traditional pattern of arranged marriages in favor of love marriages.

In Terman's famous fifty-year study of the gifted, a comparison in adulthood of those men who conspicuously failed to fulfill their early promise with those who did fulfill it showed that the successful had more self-confidence, fewer background disabilities, and were less nervous and emotionally unstable. But, he concluded, "the disadvantages associated with lower social and home status appeared to present the outstanding handicap."

The fact that women do have lower social status than men in our society and that both sexes tend to value men and male characteristics, values, and activities more highly than those of women has been noted by many authorities, including William J. Goode. What has not been done is to make the connection between this status and its accompanying personality.

The failure to extensively analyze the effects and the causes of lower social status is surprising in light of the many efforts that have been made to uncover distinct psychological differences between men and women to account for the tremendous disparity in their social production and creativity. The Goldberg study implies that even if women did achieve on a par with men it would not be perceived or accepted as such and that a woman's work must be of a much higher quality than that of a man to be given the same recognition. But these circumstances alone, or the fact that it is the male definition of achievement which is applied, are not sufficient to account for the lack of social production. So research has turned to male/female differences.

Most of this research, in the Freudian tradition, has focused on finding the psychological and developmental differences supposedly inherent in feminine nature and function. Despite all these efforts, the general findings of psychological testing indicate that: (1) Individual differences are greater than sex differences; i.e. sex is just one of the many characteristics which define a human being. (2) Most differences in ability in any field do not appear until elementary school age or later. "Sex differences become more apparent with increasing education even if it is coeducation," states Leona Tyler.

An examination of the literature of intellectual differences between the sexes discloses some interesting patterns. First, the statistics themselves show some regularity. Most conclusions of what is typical of one sex or the other are founded upon the performances of two thirds of the subjects. For example, two thirds of all boys do better on the math section of the College Board Exam than the verbal, and two thirds of the girls do better on the verbal than the math. Robert F. Bales' studies show a similar distribution when he concludes that in small groups men are the task-oriented leaders and women are the social-emotional leaders. Not all tests show this two-thirds differential, but it is the mean about which most results of the ability tests cluster. Sex is an easily visible, differentiable and testable criterion on which to draw conclusions; but it doesn't explain the one third that doesn't fit. The only characteristic virtually all women seem to have in common, besides their anatomy, is their lower social status.

Second, girls get off to a very good start. They begin speaking, reading, and counting sooner. They articulate more clearly and put words into sentences earlier. They have fewer reading and stuttering problems. Girls are even better in math in the early school years. Consistent sex differences in favor of boys do not appear until high-school age,

Eleanor Maccoby reports. Here another pattern begins to develop.

During high school, girls' performance in school and on ability tests begins to drop, sometimes drastically. Although well over half of all high-school graduates are girls, significantly less than half of all college students are girls. Presumably, this should mean that a higher percentage of the better female students go on to higher education, but their performance vis-à-vis boys' continues to decline.

Girls start off better than boys and end up worse. This change in their performance occurs at a very significant point in time. It occurs when their status changes, or to be more precise, when girls become aware of what their adult status is supposed to be. It is during adolescence that peer-group pressures to be "feminine" or "masculine" increase and the conceptions of what is "feminine" and "masculine" become more narrow. It is also at this time that there is a personal drive for conformity.

One of the norms of our culture to which a girl learns to conform is that only men excel. This was evident in Beatrice Lipinski's study of "Sex-Role Conflict and Achievement Motivation in College Women," which showed that thematic pictures depicting males as central characters elicited significantly more achievement imagery than female pictures. One need only recall S. E. Asch's experiments to see how peer-group pressures, armed only with our rigid ideas about "femininity" and "masculinity" could lead to a decline in girls' performance. Asch found that some 33 percent of his subjects would go contrary to the evidence of their own senses about something as tangible as the comparative length of two lines when their judgments were at variance with those made by the other group members. All but a handful of the other 67 percent experienced tremendous trauma in trying to stick to their correct perceptions.

When we move to something as intangible as sex-role behavior and to social sanctions far greater than the displeasure of a group of unknown experimental stooges, we can get an idea of how stifling social expectations can be. It is not surprising, in light of our cultural norm that a girl should not appear too smart or surpass boys in anything, that those pressures to conform, so prevalent in adolescence, should prompt girls to believe that the development of their minds will have only negative results. The lowered self-esteem and the denigration of their own sex noted by Smith and Goldberg are a logical consequence. These pressures even affect the supposedly unchangeable IQ scores. Corresponding with the drive for social acceptance, girls' IQs drop below those of boys during high school, rise slightly if they go to college, and go into a steady and consistent decline when and if they become full-time housewives.

These are not the only consequences. Negative self-conceptions have negative effects in a manner that can only be called a self-fulfilling prophecy. They stifle motivation and channel energies into those areas that are likely to get some positive social rewards. Then those subject to these pressures are condemned for not having strived for the highest social rewards society has to offer.

A good example of this double bind is what psychologists call the "need for achievement." Achievement motivation in male college sophomores has been studied extensively. In women it has barely been looked at; women didn't fit the model social scientists set up to explain achievement in men. Girls do not seem to demonstrate the same consistent correlation between achievement and scores on achievement tests that boys do. For example, E. N. Stivers found that "nonmotivated for college" girls scored higher on achievement motivation exams than "well-motivated for college" girls. There has been little inquiry as to why this is so. The general policy followed by the researchers was that if girls didn't fit, leave them out. Nonetheless some theories have been put forward.

James Pierce postulated that part of the confusion resulted from using the same criteria of achievement for girls that were used for boys—achievement in school. Therefore, he did a study of marriage v. career orientation in high-school girls which did show a small but consistent correlation between high achievement motivation scores and marriage orientation. In 1961 he did another study which showed a very strong correlation between high achievement scores and actual achievement of marriage within a year of high-school graduation. Those who went on to college and/or did not get married had low achievement scores.

Although he unfortunately did not describe the class origins and other relevant characteristics of his study it does seem clear that the real situation is not that women do not have achievement motivation but that this motivation is directed differently from that of men. In fact, the achievement orientation of both sexes goes precisely where it is socially directed—educational achievement for boys and marriage achievement for girls. Pierce suggested that "achievement motivation in girls attaches itself not to academic performance, but rather to more immediate adult status goals. This would be a logical assumption in that academic success is much less important to achievement status as a woman than it is for a man."

He goes on to say that "girls see that to achieve in life as adult females they need to achieve in nonacademic ways, that is, attaining the social graces, achieving beauty in person and dress, finding a desirable social status, marrying the right man. This is the successful adult woman. . . . Their achievement motivations are directed toward realizing personal goals through their relationship with men. . . . Girls who are following the normal course of development are most likely to seek adult status through marriage at an early age."

Achievement for women is adult status through marriage, not success in the usual use of the word. One might postulate that both kinds of success might be possible, particularly for the highly achievement-oriented woman. But in fact the two are more often perceived as contradictory; success in one is seen to preclude success in the other.

Matina S. Horner did a study at the University of Michigan from which she postulated a psychological barrier to achievement in women. She administered a TAT word item to undergraduates that said, "After first-term finals Anne finds herself at the top of her medical school class." A similar one for a male control group used a masculine name. The results were scored for imagery of fear of success and Horner found that 65 percent of the women but only 10 percent of the men demonstrated a definite "motive to avoid success." She explained the results by hypothesizing that the prospect of success, or situations in which success or failure is a relevant dimension, are perceived as having, and in fact do have, negative consequences for women. Success in the normal sense is threatening to women. Further research confirmed that fear of social rejection and role conflict did generate a "motive to avoid success."

Terman and Tyler showed that ability differences correlate strongly with interest differences; and women have a definite interest in avoiding success. This is reinforced by peer and cultural pressures. However, many sex differences appear too early to be much affected by peer groups and are not directly related to sex-role attributes.

One such sex difference is spatial perception, or the ability to visualize objects out of their context. This is a test in which boys do better, though differences are usually not discernible before the early school years. Other tests, such as the Embedded Figures and the Rod and Frame Tests, likewise favor boys. They indicate that boys perceive more analytically, while girls are more contextual. This ability to "break set" or be "field independent" also does not seem to appear until after the fourth or fifth year.

According to Maccoby, this contextual mode of perception common to women is a distinct disadvantage for scientific production: "Girls on the average develop a somewhat different way of handling incoming information—their thinking is less analytic, more global, and more preservative —and this kind of thinking may serve very well for many kinds of functioning but it is not the kind of thinking most conducive to high-level intellectual productivity, especially in science."

Several social psychologists have postulated that the key developmental characteristic of analytic thinking is what is called early "independence and mastery training," or "whether and how soon a child is encouraged to assume initiative, to take responsibility for himself, and to solve problems by himself, rather than rely on others for the direction of his activities." In other words, analytically inclined children are those who have not been subject to what Urie Bronfenbrenner calls "over-socialization," and there is a good deal of indirect evidence that such is the case. D. M. Levy has observed that "overprotected" boys tend to develop intellectually like girls. Elizabeth S. Bing found that those girls who were good at spatial tasks were those whose mothers left them alone to solve the problems by themselves, while the mothers of verbally inclined daughters insisted on helping them. H. A. Witkin similarly found that mothers of analytic children had encouraged their initiative, while mothers of nonanalytic children had encouraged dependence and discouraged self-assertion. James Clapp commented on these studies that "this is to be expected, for the independent child is less likely to accept superficial appearances of objects without exploring them for himself, while the dependent child will be afraid to reach out on his own, and will accept appearances without question. In other words, the independent child is likely to be more *active*, not only psychologically but physically, and the physically active child will naturally have more kinesthetic experience with spatial relationships in his environment."

The qualities associated with independence training also have an effect on IQ. I. W. Sontag did a longitudinal study in which he compared children whose IQs had improved with those whose IQs had declined with age. He discovered that the child with increasing IQ was competitive, self-assertive, independent, and dominant in interaction with other children. Children with declining IQs were passive, shy, and dependent.

Maccoby commented on this study that "the characteristics associated with a rising IQ are not very feminine characteristics. When one of the people working on it was asked about what kind of developmental history was necessary to make a girl into an intellectual person, he replied, 'The simplest way to put it is that she must be a tomboy at some point in her childhood.' "

Likewise Kagan and Moss noted that "females who perform well on problems requiring analysis and complex reasoning tend to reject a traditional feminine identification." They also observed that . . . "protection of girls was associated with the adoption of feminine interests during childhood and adulthood. Maternal protection apparently 'feminized' both the boys and the girls."

However, analytic abilities are not the only ones that are valued in our society. Being person-oriented and contextual in perception are very valuable attributes for many fields where, nevertheless, very few women are found. Such characteristics are also valuable in the arts and some of the social sciences. But while women do succeed here more than in the sciences, their achievement is still not equivalent to that of men. One explanation of this, of course, is the Horner study that established a "motive to avoid success." But when one looks further it appears that there is an earlier cause here as well.

The very same early independence and mastery training that has such a beneficial effect on analytic thinking also determines the extent of one's achievement orientation, according to Marian R. Winterbottom.

Although comparative studies of parental treatment of boys and girls are not extensive, those that have been made indicate that the traditional practices applied to girls are very different from those applied to boys. Girls receive more affection, more protectiveness, more control and more restrictions. Boys are subjected to more achievement demands and higher expectations. In short, while girls are not always encouraged to be dependent per se, they are usually not encouraged to be *independent* and physically active. Bronfenbrenner concludes: "Such findings indicate that the differential treatment of the two sexes reflects in part a difference in goals. With sons, socialization seems to focus primarily on directing and constraining the boys' impact on the environment. With daughters, the aim is rather to protect the girl from the impact of environment. The boy is being prepared to mold his world, the girl to be molded by it."

The pattern is typical of girls, Bronfenbrenner maintains, and involves the risk of "oversocialization." He doesn't discuss the possible negative effects such oversocialization has on girls, but he does express his concern about what would happen to the "qualities of independence, initiative, and self-sufficiency" of boys if such training were applied to them. "While an affectional context is important for the socialization of boys, it must evidently be accompanied by and be compatible with a strong component of parental discipline. Otherwise, the boy finds himself in the same situation as the girl, who, having received greater affection, is more sensitive to its withdrawal, with the result that a little discipline goes a long way and strong authority is constricting rather than constructive."

That these variations in socialization result in variations in personality is corroborated by Stanley Schachter's studies of first and later-born children. Like girls, first children tend to be better socialized but also more anxious and dependent, whereas second children, like boys, are more aggressive and self-confident.

Bronfenbrenner concludes that the crucial variable is the differential treatment by the father and "in fact, it is the father who is especially likely to treat children of the two sexes differently." His extremes of affection, and of authority, are both deleterious. Not only do his high degrees of nurturance and protectiveness toward girls result in "oversocialization," but "the presence of strong paternal power is particularly debilitating. In short, boys thrive in a patriarchal context, girls in a matriarchal one."

His observations receive indirect support from Elizabeth Douvan who noted that "part-time jobs of mothers have a beneficial effect on adolescent children, particularly daughters. This reflects the fact that adolescents may receive too much mothering."

The importance of mothers, as well as mothering, was pointed out by Kagan and Moss. In looking at the kinds of role models that mothers provide for developing daughters, they discovered that it is those women who are looked upon as unfeminine whose daughters tend to achieve intellectually. These mothers are "aggressive and competitive women who were critical of their daughters and presented themselves to their daughters as intellectually competitive and aggressive role models. It is reasonable to assume that the girls identified with these intellectually aggressive women who valued mastery behavior."

To sum up, there seems to be some evidence that the sexes have been differentially socialized with different training practices, for different goals, and with different results. If McClelland is right in all the relationships he finds between child-rearing practices (in particular independence and mastery training), achievement-motivation scores of individuals tested, actual achievement of individuals, and indeed, the economic growth of whole societies, there is no longer much question as to why the historical achievement of women has been so low. In fact, with the dependency training they receive so early in life, the wonder is that they have achieved so much.

But this is not the whole story. Maccoby, in her discussion of the relationship of independence training to analytic abilities, notes that the girl who does not succumb to overprotection and develop the appropriate personality and behavior for her sex has a major price to pay: a price in anxiety. Or, as Kagan and Moss have noted: "The universe of appropriate behavior for males and females is delineated early in development and it is difficult for the child to cross these culturally given frontiers without considerable conflict and tension."

Some anxiety is beneficial to creative thinking, but high or sustained levels of it are damaging, Maccoby believes, "for it narrows the range of solution efforts, interferes with breaking set, and prevents scanning of the whole range of elements open to perception." This anxiety is particularly manifest in college women, and of course they are the ones who experience the most conflict between their current—intellectual—activities, and expectations about behavior in their future—unintellectual—careers.

Maccoby feels that "it is this anxiety which helps to account for the lack of productivity among those women who do make intellectual careers." The combination of social pressures, role-expectations and parental training together tell "something of a horror story. It would appear that even when a woman is suitably endowed intellectually and develops the right temperament and habits of thought to make use of her endowment, she must be fleet of foot indeed to scale the hurdles society has erected for her and to remain a whole and happy person while continuing to follow her intellectual bent."

The reasons for this horror story must by now be clearly evident. Traditionally, women have been defined as passive creatures, sexually, physically, and mentally. Their roles have been limited to the passive, dependent, auxiliary ones, and they have been trained from birth to fit these roles. However, those qualities by which one succeeds in this society are active ones. Achievement orientation, intellectuality, and analytic ability all require a certain amount of aggression.

As long as women were convinced that these qualities were beyond them, that they were inferior in their exercise and much happier if they stayed in their place, they remained quiescent under the paternalistic system of Western civilization. Paternalism was a preindustrial scheme of life, and its yoke was partially broken by the industrial revolution. With this loosening up of the social order, the talents of women began to appear.

In the eighteenth century it was held that no woman had ever produced anything worthwhile in literature with the possible exception of Sappho [Greek lyric poet]. But in the first half of the nineteenth century, feminine writers of genius flooded the literary scene. It wasn't until the end of the nineteenth century that women scientists of note appeared, and it was still later that women philosophers were found.

Only since the industrial revolution shook the whole social order have women been able to break some of the traditional bounds of society. In preindustrial societies, the family was the basic unit of social and economic organization, and women held a significant and functional role within it. This, coupled with the high birth and death rates of those times, gave women more than enough to do within the home. It was the center of production and women could be both at home and in the world at the same time. But the industrial revolution, along with decreased infant mortality, increased life span and changes in economic organization, have all but destroyed the family as the economic unit. Technological advances have taken men out of the home, and now those functions traditionally defined as female are being taken out also. For the first time in human history women have had to devote themselves to being full-time mothers in order to have enough to do.

Conceptions of society have also changed. At one time, authoritarian hierarchies were the norm and paternalism was reflective of a general social authoritarian attitude. While it is impossible to do retroactive studies on feudalistic society, we do know that authoritarianism as a personality trait does correlate strongly with a rigid conception of sex roles, and with ethnocentrism. We also know from ethnological data that there is, as explained by W. N. Stephens, a "parallel between family relationships and the larger social hierarchy. Autocratic societies have autocratic families. As the king rules his subjects and the nobles subjugate and exploit the commoners, so does husband tend to lord it over wife, father rule over son."

According to Roy D'Andrade, "another variable that appears to affect the distribution of authority and deference between the sexes is the degree to which men rather than women control and mediate property." He presented data which showed a direct correlation between the extent to which inheritance, succession, and descent-group membership were patrilineal and the degree of subjection of women.

Even today, the equality of the sexes in the family is often reflective of the economic equality of the partners. In a Detroit sample, Robert Blood and D. M. Wolfe found that the relative power of the wife was low if she did not work and increased with her economic contribution to the family.

The employment of women [asserts Blood] affects the power structure of the family by equalizing the resources of husband and wife. A working wife's husband listens to her more, and she listens to herself more. She expresses herself and has more opinions. Instead of looking up into her husband's eyes and worshiping him, she levels with him, compromising on the issues at hand. Thus her power increases and, relatively speaking, the husband's falls.

William J. Goode also noted this pattern but said it varied inversely with class status. Toward the upper strata, wives are not only less likely to work but when they do they contribute a smaller percentage of the total family income than is true in the lower classes. Reuben Hill went so far as to say "Money is a source of power that supports male dominance in the family. . . . Money belongs to him who earns it, not to her who spends it, since he who earns it may withhold it." Phyllis Hallenbeck feels more than just economic resources are involved but does conclude that there is a balance of power in every family which affects "every other aspect of the marriage—division of labor, amount of adaptation necessary for either spouse, methods used to resolve conflicts, and so forth." Blood feels the economic situation affects the whole family structure:

Daughters of working mothers are more independent, more self-reliant, more aggressive, more dominant, and more disobedient. Such girls are no longer meek, mild, submissive, and feminine like "little ladies" ought to be. They are rough and tough, actively express their ideas, and refuse to take anything from anybody else. . . . Because their mothers have set an example, the daughters get up the courage and the desire to earn money as well. They take more part-time jobs after school and more jobs during summer vacation.

Herbert Barry, M. K. Bacon, and Irvin Child did an ethnohistoriographic analysis that provides some further insights into the origins of male dominance. After examining the ethonographic reports of 110 cultures, they concluded that large sexual differentiation and male superiority occur concurrently and in "an economy that places a high premium on the superior strength and superior development of motor skills requiring strength, which characterize the male." It is those societies in which great physical strength and mobility are required for survival, in which hunting and herding, or warfare, play an important role, that the male, as the physically stronger and more mobile sex, tends to dominate. This is supported by M. E. Spiro's analysis of sex roles in an Israeli kibbutz. There, the economy was largely unmechanized and the superior average strength of the men was needed on many jobs. Thus, despite a conscious attempt to break down traditional sex roles, they began reasserting themselves, as women were assigned to the less strenuous jobs.

Although there are a few tasks which virtually every society assigns only to men or women, there is a great deal of overlap for most jobs. Virtually every task, even in the most primitive societies, can be performed by either men or women. Equally important, what is defined as a man's task in one society may well be classified as a woman's job in another. Nonetheless, the sexual division of labor is much more narrow than dictated by physical limitations, and what any one culture defines as a woman's job will seldom be performed by a man and vice versa. It seems that what originated as a division of labor based upon the necessities of survival has spilled over into many other areas and lasted long past the time of its social value. Where male strength and mobility has been crucial to social survival, male dominance and the aura of male superiority has been the strongest. The latter has been incorporated into the value structure and attained an existence of its own.

Thus, male superiority has not ceased with an end to the need for male strength. As Goode pointed out, there is one consistent element in the assignment of jobs to the sexes, even in modern societies: "Whatever the strictly male tasks are, they are defined as *more honorific* (emphasis his) . . . . Moreover, the tasks of control, management, decision, appeals to the gods—in short the higher-level jobs that typically do *not* require strength, speed or traveling far from home—are male jobs."

He goes on to comment that

this element suggests that the sexual division of labor within family and society comes perilously close to the racial or caste restrictions in some modern countries. That is, the low-ranking race, caste, or sex is defined as not being *able* to do certain types of prestigious work, but it is also considered a violation of propriety if they do it. Obviously, if women really cannot do various kinds of male tasks, no moral or ethical prohibition would be necessary to keep them from it.

Sex roles originated in economic necessities but the value attached to any one role has become a factor of sex alone. Even cross-culturally, these roles, and the attitudes associated with them, are ingrained by common socialization practices. Barry, Bacon, and Child discovered that "pressure toward nurturance, obedience and responsibility is most often stronger for girls, whereas pressure toward achievement and self-reliance is most often stronger for boys." These are the same socialization practices traditionally found in Western society. As the Barry, Bacon, and Child study showed, these socializations serve to prepare children for roles as adults that require women to stay near the home and men to go out and achieve. The greater emphasis a society places on physical strength, the greater the sex-role differentiation and the sex differences in socialization.

These sex-role differences may have served a natural function at one time, but it is doubtful that they still do so. The characteristics we observe in women and men today are a result of socialization practices that were developed for survival of a primitive society. The value structure of male superiority is a reflection of the primitive orientations and values. But social and economic conditions have changed drastically since these values were developed. Technology has reduced to almost nothing the importance of muscular strength. In fact, the warlike attitude which goes along with an idealization of physical strength and dominance is proving to be positively destructive. The value of large families has also become a negative one. Now we are concerned with the population explosion and prefer that our society produce children of quality rather than quantity. The result of all these changes is that the traditional sex roles and the traditional family structures have become dysfunctional.

To some extent, patterns of child rearing have also changed. Bronfenbrenner reports that at least middle-class parents are raising both boys and girls much the same. He noted that over a fifty-year period middle-class parents have been developing a "more acceptant, equalitarian relationship with their children." With an increase in the family's social position, the patterns of parental treatment of children begin to converge. He likewise noted that a similar phenomenon is beginning to develop in lower-class parents and that equality of treatment is slowly working its way down the social ladder.

These changes in patterns of child rearing correlate with changes in relationships within the family. Both are moving toward a less hierarchical and more egalitarian pattern of living.

As Blood has pointed out,

today we may be on the verge of a new phase in American family history, when the companionship family is beginning to manifest itself. One distinguishing characteristic of this family is the dual employment of husband and wife. . . . Employment emancipates women from domination by their husbands and, secondarily, raises their daughters from inferiority to their brothers. . . . The classic differences between masculinity and femininity are disappearing as both sexes in the adult generation take on the same roles in the labor market. . . . The roles of men and women are converging for both adults and children. As a result the family will be far less segregated internally, far less stratified into different age generations and different sexes. The old asymmetry of male-dominated, female-serviced family life is being replaced by a new symmetry.

All these data indicate that several trends are converging at about the same time. Our value structure has changed from an authoritarian one to a more democratic one, though our social structure has not yet caught up. Social attitudes begin in the family; only a democratic family can raise children to be citizens in a democratic society. The social and economic organization of society which kept women in the home has likewise changed. The home is no longer the center of society. The primary male and female functions have left it and there is no longer any major reason for maintaining the large sex-role differentiations which it supported. The value placed on physical strength which reinforced the dominance of men, and the male superiority attitudes that this generated, have also become dysfunctional. It is the mind, not the body, which must now prevail, and woman's mind is the equal of man's. The "Pill" has liberated women from the uncertainty of childbearing, and with it the necessity of being attached to a man for economic support. But our attitudes toward women, and toward the family, have not changed concomitantly with the other developments. There is a distinct "cultural lag." Definitions of the family, conceptions of women and ideas about social function are left over from an era when they were necessary for social survival. They have persisted into an era in which they are no longer viable. The result can only be called severe role dysfunctionality for women.

The necessary relief for this dysfunctionality must come through changes in the social and economic organization of society and in social attitudes which will permit women to play a full and equal part in the social order. With this must come changes in the family, so that men and women are not only equal, but can raise their children in a democratic atmosphere. These changes will not come easily, nor will they come through the simple evolution of social trends. Trends do not move all in the same direction or at the same rate. To the extent that changes are dysfunctional with each other they create problems. These problems must be solved not by complacency but by conscious human direction. Only in this way can we have a real say in the shape of our future and the shape of our lives.

THERE ARE SEX DIFFERENCES IN THE MIND, TOO [2]

Few of the brickbats that have recently been sailing through the fragile greenhouses of our society have sprayed out more flinders of emotion and self-doubt than the Women's Liberation movement. With so many sharp edges flying about, it is understandable that some important distinctions have been generally overlooked. The many-faceted movement embraces a diversity of contentions, with very different implications for both women and men. The demands put forward by many of the feminists—probably the majority— seem quite reasonable: changes in male-oriented attitudes and arrangements so that women can enter upon and advance in a greater variety of careers and, if they wish, combine these careers with motherhood. Progress in these di-

[2] From article by Tom Alexander, an associate editor of *Fortune*. *Fortune*. 58:76-9. F. '71. Reprinted by permission.

rections is not only possible but inevitable; and, to an extent that might surprise some of the fiercer soldiers of Women's Lib, a great many men will applaud.

But some of the more radical spokeswomen of the movement are asserting a much more questionable, and potentially much more momentous, set of contentions and claims. They maintain that innate differences in temperament and ability between men and women are nonexistent or insignificant, and that the differences in the roles performed by men and women in our society are *entirely* due to social indoctrination and discrimination. The solution proposed by many radical feminists is an "androgynous" society—one in which the treatment accorded to, and the performance expected from, males and females would be essentially identical, whether at home, at school, or at work. "For the sexes are inherently in everything alike," writes Kate Millett, one widely known philosopher of the movement, "save reproductive systems, secondary sexual characteristics, orgasmic capacity, and genetic and morphological structure."

As it happens, such assertions about fundamental alikeness are being advanced at the very time when research from many scientific fields has been converging to suggest quite the opposite—that there are some inborn differences between the sexes in temperament and inclination. The most general finding of all, to be sure, is that aside from obvious differences in anatomy, physiology, and reproductive behavior, no characteristic belongs exclusively to one sex. Some differences are much more sex-specific than others, but in general, no matter what nominally male psychological trait is under consideration, some women exceed the male norm; and vice versa for nominally female traits. Some of the uncertainty in psychology is merely about the extent of these overlaps. More of the uncertainty is about the extent to which the traits have biological or social origins or some combination of both.

Differences in behavior are evident very early in life. Male infants are generally more active than females. They cry more, sleep less, and demand more attention. Female babies, while apparently more sensitive to cold, touch, and sounds, are more passive and content. They smile more often, appear to learn more rapidly, and generally seem more mature. At the age of only twelve weeks, according to some experiments, girls look longer at pictures of faces than at geometrical figures, while boys show no preference (but later they come to prefer the geometrical forms). On the average, however, boys look longer at *all* kinds of pictures than girls do.

At so early an age, it seems, females are already expressing the preferences and behavior that, for whatever reason, will develop more completely later. Girls, research predicts, will find their satisfactions in relationships with people to a greater extent than boys. They will learn to talk earlier and more fluently, and this superiority will persist through life. They will be more concerned with having companionship than boys. They will be more docile, will strive harder to please both at home and at school.

Later on, the work women select will usually involve close interaction with people. Social scientists apply the term "nurturant" to typical female professions such as child care, teaching, nursing, or social work. The feelings and the opinions of others matter more to women than to men; words of encouragement and praise often elicit more dogged effort than the prospect of promotion. One of the persistent problems of women in careers is that as they rise to high levels they often enter realms where competition is keener and praise is rare. An even more basic female handicap in the pursuit of careers is distraction: the single overriding preoccupation of most women, psychologists agree, is marriage.

A Negative Image of Success

Rightly or wrongly, women often come to suspect that too much intellectual achievement or success in male-dominated fields can impair their marriage prospects. An examination of the attitudes of Harvard law graduates by psychologist Matina Horner revealed that the women as a group had a considerably more negative image of a successful woman lawyer than the men. Moreover, the present generation of students exhibits more, not less, of this attitude than former generations did. Horner has also found that even girls in elite colleges demonstrate a powerful "motive to avoid success" in careers. It appears to arise from what they perceive as a conflict between career success and feminine identity.

There is evidence, indeed, that women who do well in male specialties tend to be a good deal more masculine in other respects than most women—they show, for example, less interest in marriage and children. A set of experiments carried out by psychologist Brian Sutton-Smith (now at Columbia) revealed that girls who are able to work out successful strategies in ticktacktoe—which is usually a male specialty—also display personality traits of an aggressive and domineering sort, more so even than boys who quickly get the hang of ticktacktoe.

Stanford psychologist Eleanor Maccoby, who herself has combined motherhood (three children) and top achievement in a male-dominated field, deplores the current low status accorded to motherhood. "We've had twenty-five years of derogating momism. While we ought to leave the doors open to those who don't choose motherhood, I would also like to see more respect for those who do." She also deplores the strains imposed upon women who enter intellectual fields. What they encounter "is something of a horror story," she says. "It would appear that even when a woman is suitably endowed intellectually and develops the right temperament and habits of thought to make use of her endowment, she must be fleet of foot indeed to scale the hurdles the society has erected for her and to remain a whole and happy person while continuing to follow her intellectual bent."

In contrast to girls, boys will maintain and develop their early dissatisfactions and quarrelsomeness and their greater interest in "things." They will give their teachers more trouble and get lower grades through high school. They will tumble and wrestle more; they will instigate catastrophes involving blocks and toy cars, and ultimately real automobiles and real implements of war. Economic considerations aside, males will work more often than females for victory over others, for power, or for achievement in workmanship or intellect. When they work for approval it will often be for those peculiar forms called prestige or fame or glory. And no matter what level they attain, males will be less content with it than their female counterparts. In short, their drive and persistence and self-motivation are likely to be greater; and, psychological experiments show, they are likely to be spurred by competition and difficulty rather than discouraged by it as females tend to be.

Tests of particular mental abilities sometimes show striking disparities between the sexes. Only about one girl in twenty, for example, demonstrates the boys' average level of ability at mechanical aptitude or certain kinds of spatial reasoning, such as is required for solving mazes. And only one male in five equals the average female in ability to perform certain kinds of perceptual tasks involving accuracy and rapid shifts of attention in the face of monotony.

Among characteristics in which the sexes show the *smallest* differences is intelligence, as measured by ordinary IQ tests. One thing often overlooked, however, is that this indistinguishability is a deliberate artifact of the tests themselves. The test compilers, from Alfred Binet on, found that males tended to score better on certain kinds of test items, such as those calling for a wide store of information or for arithmetical or spatial reasoning. Girls, on the other hand, consistently excelled on items involving symbol manipulation (as in encoding) and recognition of similarities between different things. On virtually all standard IQ tests in use today, the mix of such items is deliberately adjusted to equalize the average male and female scores.

Beyond Nature Versus Nurture

Despite wide agreement that differences exist, the social and behavioral sciences have been sharply—often emotionally—divided over whether the differences are biological or social in origin. "Science really hasn't answered the question of nature versus nurture," comments University of California psychologist Frank Beach, a longtime investigator of sex differences. "This probably means that the question has never been asked properly." But at least it is becoming clear that "nature versus nurture" is the wrong formulation. The current trend is away from contentions that sex differences are entirely attributable to nature *or* to nurture. What goes on, it appears, is a complex interaction between the two.

Until roughly a hundred years ago, scarcely anyone questioned the assumption that along with their obviously inherited bodily differences, the two sexes had inherited differences in temperament and intellect as well. But in the last decades of the nineteenth century there emerged a basic shift to the opposite view. Egalitarianism, coeducation, the feminist revolt, and the high achievements of women in male fields began chopping the ground out from under male claims to a God-given dominance and superiority. Pavlov's revealing experiments in the phenomenon of conditioning and the subsequent rise of the behavioral psychologists' views of the child as *tabula rasa*—the "blank slate" upon which over time the environment writes—led psychologists, anthropologists, sociologists, and popular opinion to view innate sex differences as insignificant and to emphasize cultural influences.

For a long time these views amounted to dogma. Frank Beach sums up the way things were:

When I was a graduate student in the early thirties the problem of sex differences was extremely sensitive, as it is today. At that time the psychologists were all environmentalists, and it was simply unthinkable to say that the sexes could differ psychologically for any reason except conditioning. Nobody argued that a woman's size, general body formation, or reproductive anatomy were not strongly influenced by genetic factors. But the curtain dropped when it got to psychology, as though the brain, which controls behavior, was totally unaffected. I can recall getting scolded when I even raised the issue, because if you said that boys and girls differed, it seemed automatically to mean that one was inferior and the other superior. Even then tests were coming out showing that boys did better in math and girls did better in English, but if you ever suggested that this kind of thing had genetic origins at all it somehow suggested that girls were inferior. Why English should be inferior to math, I don't know.

By now, however, most adherents of the environmental explanation of sex differences have shifted away from older behaviorist ideas that externally imposed reward and punishment—i.e., approval or disapproval by parents or society— were the principal shapers of male or female personality. Now widely held is the "role modeling" theory, which stresses some sort of motivation in the individual to shape himself according to the society's prevailing stereotypes. Once a child begins to identify itself as male or female—that seldom happens before the age of eighteen months, psychologists think—it is driven to search the world around it for clues as to how to assemble a personality appropriate to its sex and culture. In effect, this need to establish an "identity" is akin to the innate and irrepressible drive to learn the culture's language.

Both science and common sense lead inescapably to the conclusion that some form of role modeling is a major shaper of personality. The roles of the sexes differ widely from one culture to another. Among the Tchambuli of New Guinea, the males are raised to be passive and emotionally dependent. Anthropologists who studied a large number of cultures found that in more than half of them the accepted role of women included doing practically all the heavy carrying. In some West African societies women control much of the commerce. Even modern nations show striking

differences in the extent to which women do various kinds
of work. In the USSR, for example, some 75 percent of the
medical doctors are women.

The Beat of Inner Drums

Even so, any simple version of the role-modeling hypothesis faces certain logical difficulties that clearly point to
limits in the malleability of the sexes. One problem, for
instance, is that traits such as male aggressiveness or female
verbal superiority display themselves at a very early age,
presumably long before the child knows which parent to
imitate. Similarly, it seems unlikely that, for example, male
children are able to discern subtle differences in their parents' intellectual styles by the early age at which males begin
to evidence signs of their superiority at spatial reasoning.
So, while males and females need to respond to their culture's
peculiar orchestration, they hear the beat of inner drums
as well.

Two developments in the 1950s helped to breed a new
industry of speculative writing about innate components
of behavior. One was the flowering of ethology, the study
of animal behavior. The other was the discovery in Africa
of fossil remains indicating that man is a direct descendant
of weapon-wielding, tool-using, ground-living, hunting primates whose emergence may date as far back as twenty
million years or more. Putting together findings from these
two areas of research, a number of scientists have concluded
that much more of human behavior may have genetic roots
than was previously imagined.

For the closest living analogues to mankind's predeces-
sors, scientists have looked to other primate species. Virtually
all of the ground-dwelling primates have some sort of social
structure in which the leaders are male. Because of their
vulnerability to predators, baboons and rhesus and Japanese
macaque monkeys appear to have evolved defensive cultures
complete with intricate hierarchies of dominance and sub-

mission and considerable differentiation in sex roles and traits. In general, a groundling primate troop of whatever size has a single dominant leader (ethologists refer to him as the "alpha" male), with lesser males arrayed in a rank order beneath him. The male hierarchy favors organized action for the defense of the females and their young.

It is a notable aspect of these primate societies that the basic social format of each species is transmitted at least partly in the form of a genetic program, a program that permits a limited range of variations in behavior to accommodate changes in the environment. The definitive experiments have yet to be carried out, but there is suggestive evidence that if infant members of these "culture-forming" primates are placed together before they have had a chance to learn the society's norms, they will nevertheless eventually sort themselves into a fair copy of the social order characteristic of their species.

Primate young also display behavioral sex differences that appear to be innate. Males are more aggressive and indulge more in playful sexual mounting. Females perform more "grooming" of other members and show more interest in still younger infants.

As a ground-dwelling primate, man must have received a good deal of genetic programming from many millions of years of hunting ancestors. Though wide variations in behavior patterns are evident in various cultures, there do appear to be quite a few cultural "universals" for the human species. The most obvious, probably, are male dominance and aggression and, of course, female nurturance, or maternalism. Despite much speculation in fable and feminist literature about matriarchal—i.e., female-governed—societies, there is no evidence that such have ever really existed. There have been, and are, quite a few "matrilineal" cultures, in which descent is reckoned by the blood line of the female, but even in these societies governance is largely or entirely a male domain.

Man, the Domesticated Animal

Those who emphasize innate sex differences often encounter the objection that it is useless or deluding to try to extrapolate from the ethological or fossil evidence to human behavior. "In general," cautions Frank Beach, "the higher you go on the evolutionary scale, the more behavior is determined by environmental factors and learning than by biological influence directly. Susceptibilities and predispositions may be genetic; complex behavior patterns are probably not."

The well-known ethologist, Konrad Lorenz, contends that humans are more closely analogous to domesticated animals than to wild animals. Usually, wild animals express their genetically transmitted behavior in direct, unambiguous ways. But in a state of domestication, those adaptations that were once necessary for survival in a perilous environment are gradually bred out or distorted or become dangerously inappropriate, as may be the case with the human will to violence.

Nevertheless, like many other ethologists, Lorenz believes that a large and perhaps dominant source of our behavior is genetic or instinctual. Even when it does not express itself in the complicated behavior patterns of lower species, it shows up in propensities, mainly as strong emotions—such as love, anger, maternalism, and probably yearnings to dominance or affiliation as well. Most of these propensities in humans, it is true, can be modified or overridden by cultural influences. But a persistent question keeps occurring to ethologists and psychiatrists: What are the costs—to the individual and to society—of overriding them? Do these costs, for example, include what in some instances we mean by neurosis?

Altered in the Womb

Major contributions to the understanding of sex differences have come from the field of endocrinology. Scientists have long known that sex hormones—the female hormones, such as progesterone and various estrogens, and the male hormones or androgens such as testosterone—must be involved in behavior. But prior to puberty, it is thought, roughly equal amounts of androgens and estrogens are present in the blood stream of male and female children alike, and this originally lent support to the role-modeling theorists' views that whatever differences in behavior were to be found in children must be due to learning.

Beginning in the 1950s, however, animal experiments have clearly shown that not only anatomical differences between males and females but also certain aspects of male and female behavior are determined prior to birth. In the late fifties, for example, a group of University of Kansas scientists, including Charles Phoenix, Robert Goy, and the late William Young, injected female guinea pigs with small amounts of masculinizing hormone before birth and found that the animals' anatomical and behavioral futures could thereby be altered for all their lives. That is to say, these genetic females proceeded to develop not only the genitalia but also the mating behavior typical of males. Subsequent experiments have revealed that the same effects hold for animals higher than the guinea pig.

The fundamental organization of mammalian brains and bodies, it appears, is female first and only secondarily male, a reversal of the sequence assumed in the story of Adam and Eve. In human fetuses during the early stages of gestation, the brain of either sex possesses, in effect, the "blueprints" and latent neural circuits to develop and behave either as a female or a male. But if left hormonally alone, the fetus will always develop into a female. What happens in the case of males is that the male sex chromosome triggers a brief spurt of androgen from the fetal gonads. This spurt, in turn, somehow triggers a chain of chemical and organizational events that result in maleness. These include activating the neural circuits that will generate masculine behavioral propensities in the later presence of male hormones.

The female circuits, however, are not completely turned off; they continue to make a greater or lesser contribution to the behavior of even a "normal" male all through life. Experiments with rats, for instance, have shown that even a normal adult male rat can be induced to simulate female mating and maternal behavior by injections of hormones at certain sites in the brain. The reverse holds for females.

An Unhappy Bunch of Boys

Recent experiments reveal not only how the sex hormones influence the behavior of individual rhesus and macaque monkeys but also how the very composition of the monkey "culture" is partly subject to the hormonal balance of one or two individuals. These experiments were conducted at the Oregon Regional Primate Research Center near Portland, one of seven federally funded research centers set up in the United States to take experimental advantage of the kinship between monkeys and men. Psychologists Goy and Phoenix, who had taken part in the pioneering experiments at Kansas, are now at the Oregon center. They and several of their colleagues have altered the direction of development of fetal female monkeys by means of male hormone injections prior to birth. After birth these masculinized females behave more like males than females. That is to say, from infancy onward they indulge in much of the rough-and-tumble play and threatening grimaces of males of their species, as well as imitating the male-type infantile mating play.

It sometimes happens that by dint of sheer aggressiveness one of these masculinized females will work her way up to become the "alpha" individual in her troop. So far as human observers are able to judge, the members of these troops are quite happy with their unorthodox leaders. But the results of some other hormone experiments at the Oregon center have been less happy for the monkey communities involved. In one study, instead of masculinizing the fetus, a researcher has injected male hormones into normal females after birth but prior to puberty. These monkeys too become aggressive, and sometimes one emerges into alpha status. The day this happens is a dark one for the males; from that time on she absolutely prohibits her male subjects from playing their rough-and-tumble games or engaging in their mock-sexual play. "She makes the boys sit quietly in the corners," says Goy, "and they're obviously a very unhappy bunch of boys."

These experiments with guinea pigs, rats, and monkeys clearly signal that temperament is related to sex hormones. Recent research reveals that this is true of people too. At Johns Hopkins Hospital, for example, psychologists John Money and Anke Ehrhardt have investigated several varieties of human hermaphroditism—ambiguities in sexual development. Hermaphroditism occurs in a fetus because of some congenital inability of the cells to respond to sex hormones, or because of hormone therapy to the mother during pregnancy. Occasionally, therefore, a genetic male is born indistinguishable in infantile appearance from a female (though possessing no uterus and with internal testes in place of ovaries). Naturally, parents often unknowingly raise these infants as girls. Usually, these children grow up happily into women. They may like dolls, they often date boys, and they frequently marry. Though sterile, of course, they adopt children and display normal maternal affection.

Mysterious Programs

Initially, evidence of this kind was seen by some psychologists as support for the view that social upbringing was the all-important shaper of behavior. But later studies by Money and others now suggest a different interpretation: in the feminized-male hermaphrodite, the brain as well as the body has failed to receive the normal hormonal stimulation toward maleness. Support for this view comes from investigation of another form of hermaphroditism. It involves genetic females who because of therapy or a glandular malfunction are supplied before birth with excessive amounts of androgen-like substances after their ovaries and female internal reproductive organs are already formed, but before the external genitalia have stopped developing. In many such cases, surgery and hormone treatments can be employed early to bring about the development of a completely normal-appearing fertile female. But this intervention apparently comes too late to offset completely the effects on the brain. The girls often act more like boys than girls. They tend to display an unusual degree of interest in outdoor athletics, a preference for boys' toys instead of dolls, and even a pattern, in Money's words, of "giving priority to career over marriage or at least combining the two in future expectancies."

Very early in the development of any human being, the evidence suggests, the presence of minute amounts of one hormone or the other activates some as yet mysterious program that, together with later hormonal activity, will partly determine what kinds of experiences and social molding a given individual will tend to prefer, ignore, or reject. Some researchers go further and propose that differences in cognitive "style" between males and females are traceable to hormonal influences upon the central nervous system. Psychologists Donald and Inge Broverman, a husband and wife team who work at Worcester State Hospital in Massachusetts, draw upon a great deal of psychological and biochemical research in arguing the controversial hypothesis that such intellectual differences . . . are due to the differential stimulating effects of male and female hormones upon different nervous subsystems.

Why Women Feel Hurt

The Brovermans maintain that estrogen increases the acuteness of many sensory perceptions. This may account for the observations reported by various researchers that females tend to show more acute hearing, taste, and tactile sense than males. By the same token, according to Broverman, this lower sensory threshold may also cause most women to hurt more under punishment, and to have a greater need than most men to avoid stressful situations. From an evolutionary standpoint this would make sense, for lower levels of fear and sensitivity to pain would be of benefit to males engaged in the rigors of hunt or combat.

The greater sensitivity of women leads Broverman to speculate that females can be conditioned more quickly to respond to stimuli than males. This might help explain some of the male puzzlement at the feminist contentions that our patriarchal society will not "let" women practice male pursuits and occupations. The explanation may be that women tend to respond to the conditioning pressures of society more acutely than do men.

Better Living Through Chemistry?

The large and growing body of evidence of the existence of inborn differences in temperament between men and women does not deny the validity of feminist demands for changes in existing social arrangements. All aspects of society should be subject to reexamination and readjustment to ensure that all citizens enjoy the right to optimal development of their human potentialities. But Kate Millett was much too dolorous when she wrote: "If human sexual temperament is inherent, there is really very little hope for us."

Indeed, innate differences need not stand in the way even of the homogenized androgyny that some radical feminists call for. If that were what society really wanted, it might one day be possible to use hormone pills to make males and females think and behave very much alike. (A side effect might be to suppress women's menstrual cycle, which has pervasive debilitating effects. A British study reports, for example, that school girls' performance on written examinations declines by roughly 15 percent during the few days prior to menstruation.) A more efficient approach to androgyny would be to intervene in the early stages of pregnancy when the male or female neural circuits were being activated. By means of hormone implantations or deletions in this period, it should be perfectly feasible to masculinize the female fetus or feminize the male. The society thus created would be undeniably androgynous, and—most people would agree—awful.

Short of such measures, education and social pressures could undoubtedly bring about a considerable narrowing of the differences between the roles of the two sexes. Several educational researchers have demonstrated that special encouragement can offset much of women's lack of interest or ability in certain kinds of creative problem solving. It also seems clear that social influences can reduce overt male aggressiveness.

Competing at Men's Own Games

It is far from clear, however, that the use of training and indoctrination to make the sexes behave more alike would foster optimal satisfaction for either males or females. Edward Zigler, formerly a psychologist at Yale and now director of the Federal Office of Child Development, puts the matter this way:

All that behavior geneticists have taught us suggests that genetic variation is an important component in many of the male-female behavioral differences we observe. Perhaps many of these genetically influenced behavioral differences could be overridden through training, but only at some considerable psychological cost. I think that such a thing as being true to one's self makes sense genetically as well as making for a much more interesting society.

What does seem clear is that deliberate blindness toward the evidence of innate differences is likely to lead to greater strains and dissatisfactions among women—and men as well. So long as feminists measure their progress in terms of how well they as a class compete with men at men's own games, their cause is likely to be damaging to women's self-esteem. For there will always be fewer high-ranking jobs than there are people who want them, and society has found no effective —or fair—way of filling them except through some kind of competition. Individual women, of course, should be free to decide which of these kinds of games they want to play, as well as how hard. But given the psychological evidence on male needs for achievement, together with the female distractions of marriage and maternity, it seems likely that there will always be more men than women at the top.

On the other hand, the importance of men's special traits may be on the decline. Aggression, preoccupation with technology, even competitive ambition itself, seem to be counting for less and less as our society matures. Conversely, the especially feminine qualities of nurturance and concern for people may be assuming more importance in a society threatened with disintegration. If in their quest for a more androgynous world, feminists lop off the feminine end of the behavioral spectrum, the operation could well be fatal.

THE QUESTION OF PSYCHOLOGICAL DIFFERENCES BETWEEN THE SEXES [3]

This question seems particularly relevant in these times when roles for both sexes are changing and when so many of our national problems are going from bad to worse.

I'm convinced that we will only be able to save our world if we can understand ourselves a lot better than we have in the past—including the attitudes and behavior of each sex. Then we could foster those of our aspirations that are socially valuable, and curb or sublimate the ones that are destructive. Here are three examples: (1) Men must be more aware that the various expressions of their need to prove virility are not heroic but suicidal traits in a nuclear age. (2) Our society, if it is to turn away from excessive materialism and competitiveness, will need to recruit millions into the caring professions which many men have avoided because these were considered untraditional for males (e.g., elementary school teaching, social work, nursing), and which women have often shunned because so few

[3] From *Decent and Indecent; Our Personal and Political Behavior*, by Benjamin Spock, M.D. rev. ed. Fawcett. '71. Reprinted by permission of the McCall Publishing Company. © 1969, 1970, 1971 by James M. Houston, Trustee, under an Irrevocable Trust dated October 6, 1966, between Benjamin M. Spock of Cleveland, Ohio, Donor, and James M. Houston of Pittsburgh, Pennsylvania, Trustee.

men were in them. (3) The tendency of many males to depersonalize their occupational and family relationships, which limits their effectiveness, could be counteracted through appropriate teaching and training methods.

The average boy shows more restlessness, tenseness, and combative aggressiveness right from birth, I think. Between one and three years he is more resistant to toilet training. Boys get lower grades in school and college because they are inclined to balk and argue, aloud or silently; this sometimes keeps them from hearing what the instructor is saying. Even at two or three years they sense the general spirit of pistol play, long before they have any knowledge of death or ballistics. They continue to play cowboy or soldier with sparkling eyes and barking guns until they are nearly adolescent, an occupation that very few girls can be drawn into, even in the family in which the parents would have no objection.

Girls at an ice rink skate sociably with each other or practice spins. Boys persistently and illegally skate against the current and play tag in and out amongst the nervous adults, enjoying the combat with each other and the indignation of the older people.

Women on the average have more agreeableness in the inborn core of their personality, I think, though of course this can be counteracted when they are brought up in a situation that encourages aggressiveness or hostility.

Though a boy or man is more aggressive, he is also designed to accept the curbing of his aggressiveness. More exactly, his aggressiveness can be turned inside out and becomes his law-abidingness. This disciplining takes place to the extent that he is raised in a society and in a family that is concerned with the civilizing of aggressiveness. There have been tribes in which the males preyed fiercely on other tribes, fought with fellow tribesmen, bullied their women. In our own kind of civilization there are neighborhoods (shrinking now) where men brawl frequently and have little respect for the law or women. At the opposite extreme (leaving out the effeminate man, who is a special case) might be the kind

of professor, for example, in whom no aggressiveness what-
soever is detectable, who is steered around at home by his
wife, and who would have a horror of breaking any law or
regulation.

Erik Erikson in a revealing experiment presented small
dolls representing adults and children, dolls' furniture, toy
cars, building blocks to a series of American school-age boys
and girls. He asked each one to set the stage and indicate a
scenario for a movie about an exciting occurrence. Boys built
towering structures with the blocks—a characteristic assertion of manliness—and then usually depicted a scene of violence, most commonly a burglary or a traffic accident.
Policemen were used almost invariably, to arrest the culprit.
So boys are preoccupied with aggression but equally with
the need to control it.

Girls would use the blocks, if at all, to outline the rooms
in a house. They would arrange the furniture by rooms.
Then they placed members of the family in conventional
domestic situations.

A good example of the conversion of aggression into
cooperation occurs in automobile driving. There are insecure men who criticize women for being terrible drivers.
They can't be referring to the statistics on accidents or
deaths because these show that the dangerous drivers are
mainly men, asserting their hostile competitiveness and their
virility in a perilous manner. The critical males are referring,
for instance, to the woman driver who doesn't think to get
into the left lane before making a left turn or the right lane
for a right turn. The kind of man who is always in the
correct lane is there because his inborn aggression, inverted
into cooperativeness by strict parental training, is constantly
reminding him to be considerate. Many a man in the wrong
lane is there because his aggressiveness was never well curbed.
The woman in the wrong lane is rarely a ruthless or even
an inconsiderate person; her nonautomotive life shows this.
There is not enough hostility in her makeup to worry her
conscience.

The emotional strengths that women contribute in abundance to society are, I think, realism, sensibleness, personalness. They are clearly aware of the human relationships around them. They have a strong urge to satisfy human needs.

When a case in the courts is settled in a way that accords with legal logic but is grossly unfair as applied in a specific case, a woman cries out impatiently, "How absurd!" But her husband, ready to be seduced by theory, says, "Don't you see that the law *has* to take this position, even if it causes injustice?"

Men more often than women have a drive to schematize and intellectualize. They are inclined to forget about the immediate, the real aspects of a problem in the family or at work—and to become absorbed in some theoretical aspect of it. They can ignore the wholeness of a situation and focus on one particular element. They can shut out the personal and emotional aspects of even a human relations problem in trying to analyze it in abstract terms. They are fascinated with machines partly because a machine is an impersonal and generalized means for carrying out an act. Even at a year of age more boy babies seem to me to be fascinated with the manipulation of a machine such as the doctor's ear light.

This tendency to drift from the real to the abstract is, in part, drilled into boys and girls by the overintellectuality of many homes and schools. Freud ascribed it, in developmental terms, to the suppression of the feelings, especially the romantic feelings, of the child toward his parent at the time of the resolution of the Oedipus complex. I think that the compulsion to suppress feelings is stronger on the average in boys in part because their Oedipal anxiety is greater. . . . Girls can also be made impersonal but it takes more mental disciplining by sternly intellectual parents and teachers to suppress their feelings. The disadvantage of this trait, in the human relations of the home or office, is the liability of many people, particularly men, to be absent-minded and impersonal. This keeps them from seeing the whole situation they are faced with and frustrates the people with whom they are dealing, whose needs and sensibilities are being ignored.

A small example of the male itch to turn an ordinary action into a system occurs at soda fountains. Women simply make sandwiches and drinks. Men turn such an occupation into a combination of game, ballet, and race against time in which they grab the bread, slap on the filling, slice, and sling the sandwich all in one rapid, sleight-of-hand sequence —meanwhile bellowing cryptic orders back and forth and slipping exaggerated compliments to their female customers.

A core problem for men is the question of the adequacy of their virility. This is a matter of only barely perceptible uncertainty for some, an incessant preoccupation—conscious or unconscious—for others. Fear of sexual impotence is its most obvious aspect; this is an ingredient of a large proportion of all jibes and dirty stories, and a common cause of infidelity on the part of men trying to prove themselves to themselves.

The striving to prove virility plays a part in competition with other men for jobs, money, fame, athletic laurels, women; in the size and power of automobiles; in the inclination to boast and strut and declaim. It is demonstrated more convincingly when men stand up to each other in bargaining and fights.

Its early root (in the belief of Freud and myself) is the small boy's increasing awareness of and resentment about his father's impressive genital head start. This phallic focus of rivalry becomes a part of the boy's competitiveness with other boys; it shows up in frequent locker room kidding about the smallness or largeness of different boys' genitals and in competition for distance in urinating.

Each male's concern about his virility continues throughout boyhood and manhood and is affected by all the other vicissitudes of his life. His assurance is increased by any kind of material success, or honors, by the depth of his wife's pride and appreciation, by the respect of men and women generally, as well as by his genital potency. Of course most men limit the risk of failure by carefully trimming their ambitions to their capabilities.

In the same category but infinitely more dangerous is man's fear of losing face and his reluctance to admit publicly that he has made a mistake. (Societies and individuals differ a lot in this regard.) Families have been ruined and nations have been dragged through frightful wars to save men these discomforts.

When men can't establish an aura of authoritativeness by legitimate means, they may try to do it with pomposity. (They do this less often now in the United States because pomposity is made fun of here.) The fear of not being accorded authority must have a lot to do with men marrying women two or three years their juniors, all over the world.

In many societies boys are taught that it is shameful to cry, to appear weak, to act fearful, or perhaps even to show feelings of any kind. When men try to conceal their fearfulness with boldness, they often get into trouble. Shame about showing feeling sometimes makes a man so insensitive to all the feelings of other people, as well as to his own, that he is very difficult for family, friends, coworkers to live with.

Related to the fear of seeming weak is the impulse to court danger. There's a psychological mechanism called libidinization of pain: When a person, particularly in childhood, is subjected to an emotionally painful situation over a period of years, he comes to get a perverse kind of pleasure from it. Without conscious realization, he seeks to repeat it thereafter. A boy forces himself repeatedly to face danger in order to prove to himself and to the world that he is not afraid. At first this is almost as painful to him as it would be to a girl. But as the months and years pass he receives a pleasurable excitement from it.

When a child falls through the ice from venturing out where he was forbidden to go, it is practically always a boy. When a child is caught halfway up a cliff, unable to climb up or down, it's always a boy. It's men who keep attempting the Himalayas. A great majority of women see danger simply and realistically as something to be avoided; only a few have been taught to enjoy it.

Men's readiness to take chances to prove their courage, which sometimes drives their wives to distraction, does have value. It is of course one of the main sources of the boldness with which they circumvent difficulties, defy traditions, change jobs, endure hardship.

Another aspect of the fear of weakness is the reluctance to ask for help. In psychiatry it's called "fear of dependency." A man driving a car in the country is obviously lost. His wife says, "There's a farmer; let's ask him the way." The husband brushes this suggestion aside, "I'm pretty sure the road I'm looking for is just ahead." Twenty minutes later they are still lost, the wife makes the same suggestion and the husband makes the same reply.

The fear of being effeminate or homosexual is another subdivision. European observers have been struck by how particularly strong this dread is in America. The psychiatrist can explain that such fears are conscious or unconscious recognition of inner tendencies to effeminacy or homosexuality. But this tells little because all men are believed to have some degree of both; and a burly athlete may show more intolerance than a gentle scholar. So we end up saying only that some men are much more rigid, perfectionistic, and insecure about their virility than others.

Women often criticize men or laugh at them for being cowards because they meekly bow to customs and obligations of questionable validity. Many a man when uncertain whether to tip would much rather tip than not. He would rather tip too much than run the risk of tipping too little. A similar situation galling to wives is the contributions men are asked to make at their places of work—to charities, to testimonials, to political candidacies. This is partly a matter of submissiveness; I suspect that there are more men who are afraid of angering other men—particularly those in authority such as the boss, the policeman, the judge—than there are women in awe of other women—the woman boss, the school principal, the social leader of the community. (Few adults of either sex are scared of people of the opposite sex.) One underlying cause, in the unconscious, is that males assume in early childhood that they have a lot to fear from their fathers, while most girls assume they have little further to fear from their mothers.

Men also bow to custom because they are afraid of being thought inexperienced, innocent.

I myself believe, from pediatric and other observations, that there are quantitative differences of drive between the average man and woman and that these differences are based not only on marked differences in the way they have been treated since birth but also on inborn temperament. The latter have been built into the two sexes during the long evolution of our species, like the differences in size and shape, because men and women had different jobs to do. Our remote ancestors came down out of the trees to live by hunting and fighting. The male had to develop aggressiveness, chance-taking, bravado. He had to build weapons, houses, machines; so he evolved with a greater average drive to invent, build, and theorize.

Women have predominantly cared for their families, prepared the food, and made the clothes. So they have remained more attuned to human needs and feelings; and more conservative in the sense of less rash.

I don't believe that all girls are born with the same temperament, or all boys. There are distinct inborn differences between individuals of each sex, which one can see clearly in fraternal twins of the same sex. But I think that the innate temperament of a hundred girls, when averaged, will differ from that of a hundred boys.

There is considerable overlap. For example, among a hundred girls there may be a few who have more inborn aggressiveness than the average boy; and, among a hundred boys, a few who have less than the average girl.

People who take the opposite view from mine point to all the studies showing how markedly the personality characteristics of different groups are formed by cultural pressures. I concede the enormous influence of parents and society. Psychiatry operates on this assumption. I also admit from the start that I can't prove my belief: even if I collected figures showing significant temperamental differences at six months of age, a skeptic could point out that these might be caused by the different ways in which parents treat boys and girls even in infancy.

Views like mine are particularly offensive to those fighting for Women's Liberation because they know that male employers excuse their discrimination against women on the basis of what they call women's feminine personality traits —"not logical" or "too emotional" are familiar clichés. (They forget the men who are "not logical" or are "too emotional.") That is not my position. I'm not justifying any discrimination or trying to dissuade any woman or man from any field, however unconventional. I believe that women and men have the qualities to work in any field that they have a mind to enter. A girl or boy who develops a strong drive to enter a field that has traditionally had few of their sex in it will, in the first place, already have a personality suited to that occupation. (For example, the woman who wants to be a brain surgeon is already cool, iron-nerved, and determined; the man who wants to be a nursery school teacher has a high sensitivity to children's feelings.) Furthermore, men and women can effectively cultivate any additional traits and capabilities considered valuable for the particular occupation that appeals to them. So the innate sex differences I think of are only tendencies, strong in one individual, faint in another. They can be fostered or counteracted, depending on society's influence and the individual's aspirations.

At the start of this discussion I said that if people of each sex could recognize more clearly their temperamental makeup they could foster the traits likely to benefit society, try to control those that are dangerous and compensate for deficiencies. Women in architecture should more often be able to be especially creative in enhancing the livability and practicality of buildings, which men have often neglected in their impulse to focus on forms. Women in law and in legislatures could be leading a crusade to humanize the desiccated statutes and the cruel procedures of the courts.

Male students in school, college, and graduate school need to be frequently steered away from the theoretical and even intolerant positions they so often take on human affairs, and brought back to how real people feel, including themselves.

FEMALE BIOLOGY IN A MALE CULTURE [4]

As a subject of conversation, Women's Liberation is certainly unequaled for putting everyone, women as well as men, in the happy state of mind that results from establishing one's superiority to whatever is benighted and ridiculous in human activity. In fact, I can think of only one other topic that matches it as a provoker of ignorant mirth among the presumably well-educated, and that is psychoanalysis— not psychiatry, which people have always recognized as a serious subject, but Freudian analysis.

The parallel should not surprise us. In both situations the derisive response represents embarrassment at being caught in a deception, and a defense against being confronted with an unwanted truth. The amusement with which, even at this late date, the mention of psychoanalysis can be met is confirmation that we do indeed have a life of the unconscious that we are fearful of bringing to consciousness. And, just so, the ready mockery of Women's Liberation is confirmation that women are indeed regarded in our society as of a second order of being, and that we are afraid of having the falseness of this assumption revealed to us. By us, of course, I mean women no less than men.

[4] Article by Diana Trilling, author and critic. *Saturady Review*. 53:16-18. O. 10, '70. Copyright 1970 Saturday Review, Inc. Reprinted by permission.

It is both appropriate and ironic that in undertaking to speak of the present movement for women's rights I bring it into such immediate conjunction with Freudian thought. The appropriateness lies in the fact that for many years my own view of the relation of the sexes was rather substantially shaped by Freud's perception of the differing biological natures of the sexes and of the consequent differences in their psychological lives and their social roles. Recently, this influence has been modified: I tend now to give more weight than I once did to the cultural, as opposed to the biological, determinism in sexual attitudes. For example, I am not as convinced as I might once have been that a woman's willingness to cede power to men necessarily represents a wholesome acceptance of her female role; now I might see it as a not very laudable cultural conformity or even an expediency or laziness. The irony of bringing Freud into immediate connection with the subject of Women's Liberation lies in Freud's having had such an invidious view of the female sex. I am afraid that the man who sought to liberate the psyche from the hindrances imposed upon it in our human infancy was interested not at all in liberating women from the special handicaps imposed upon them in our society. Nowhere in his writings does Freud express sympathy for the problems that pertain to the female sex alone. On the contrary, his misogyny is now taken for granted even by his most admiring students.

Freud's condescension toward women is rooted in his castration theory, which plays a vital part in his whole theory of neurosis. According to Freud, it is the male sexual organ that constitutes what might be called the natural, or ideal, endowment from which stems the genital envy particular to women and the anxiety shared by both sexes. And no doubt it is as an extension of this view of woman's basic biological inferiority that Freud makes his forthright statement in *Civilization and Its Discontents* that it is men who are the makers and carriers of culture. He adjures women not to interfere with man's life in culture.

The adjuration could scarcely be more irritating, especially when we contemplate some of the activities that men regard as a proper life in culture, like inventing hydrogen bombs or claiming the moon for their own country. Such being man's impulses in culture, one might have hoped that Freud would have encouraged women to tell their husbands to stay home and be sensible. On the other hand, there is nothing either in Freud's formulation of the castration fear or in his general statement of the different relation of men and women to culture that I would be prepared to fault or that people far more competent than I have succeeded in refuting. It would be pleasant, for instance, to accept the idea proposed by Dr. Karen Horney, the mother of Freudian revisionism, and so widely propagated by Margaret Mead, that womb-envy, man's envy of woman because she can have babies and he cannot, plays as much a part in the life of men as penis-envy plays in the life of women. Such an appealing reassignment of biological advantage is supported, however, neither by men's dreams nor their free associations during psychoanalytical treatment.

As to the relative roles of men and women in culture, it would seem to be indisputable, at least historically, that for better or worse men have forged the ideas and provided the chief energies by which cultures develop, while women have devoted themselves to the conservation of what they have found valuable in the efforts of men. We may protest that there is no work in culture that is as valuable as woman's childbearing and child-nurturing activities; that the ability to create and conserve the human race overshadows any other conceivable accomplishment in culture. But this, of course, begs the question of why women have not made even a small fraction of the intellectual, scientific, or artistic contributions to culture that men have made.

Finally, we may protest that women's small contribution to culture is not an indication of their capacities but simply reflects the way that men have contrived things to be—that is, we can blame women's small place in culture *on* culture

—except that this leaves unanswered the question of why it is that over the long years women have been willing that culture should follow the male dictate. It also leaves unanswered the even more fundamental question of why it is that in every society that has ever been studied—so Margaret Mead tells us—whatever it is that is the occupation of men has the greater prestige: If the men do the hunting and fighting, hunting and fighting are the status-giving occupations of that society; if the men do the weaving and baby-tending, then weaving and baby-tending are the superior activities. We may think of this value system as something that men impose upon women. But then we are forced to explain why it is that even where the women bear arms they have not imposed a different system of values.

The reference back to biology would seem to be unavoidable, and we are returned to Freud's use of the words "passivity" and "activity"—female passivity, male activity. The words themselves almost inevitably imply a judgment, especially in a culture like ours where passivity connotes unattractive attributes: inertness, laxness, the uncritical acceptance of whatever happens to be given. Even as a concept in the purely sexual relation of men and women it suggests that man is the seeker and that woman yields to man's importunities, a description of the sexual roles that is not particularly congruent with our modern sense of the sexual realities. But actually this distinction between the active and the passive sexual roles is an irrefutable fact in nature: The most active seduction or participation on the part of a woman cannot relieve the male partner of his primary physical responsibility in their sexual union. To put the matter at its crudest, the male has the biological capacity to rape; the female has not. We may, if we wish, accuse Freud of drawing too many, or mistaken, emotional and social inferences from this fundamental biological difference between the sexes, but to try to ignore the difference, as some of the Women's Liberation groups do, is to narrow rather than widen the prospects opened up to us in refusing the tyrannies of biology.

It is reported that Freud would be rather bitterly amused when accused of being dirty-minded because he wrote about infant sexuality; he would point out that it was not he who had created the condition, he had merely recognized it. And obviously he didn't create the different sexual endowments of men and women nor even the emotional consequences of the difference; he only recognized them, and attached these words "active" and "passive" to the differing sexual roles. After centuries of female subjugation, however, it was perhaps expectable that the essential lack of sympathy for women in orthodox psychoanalysis, and in particular its emphasis on women's envy of men with its implication of hostility, would be one of the aspects of Freud's thought that would be most readily received by our society. I think there is small doubt that Freudian doctrine, often scarcely understood or even misunderstood, has enormously powered the development in recent decades of what amounts to virtually an antifemale movement in American culture.

The informing sentiment of this movement is that women are out to destroy men: Women are the natural destroyers of the male species, at least in America. As statistics have been gathering on the appalling numbers of men who die from heart disease in this country, increasingly, the blame has been put on the American wife for the killing demands she makes upon her husband for houses, cars, washing machines, and clothes. She has been pictured as the ruthless exploiter of her male partner, a sort of prototypical domestic statement of the national imperialism. And as Freud's views on the childhood source of mental disorder have percolated into the culture, there has been mounted a growing campaign of mother-suspicion and mother-discreditation. From Sidney Howard's play *The Silver Cord*, in the mid-twenties, to Philip Roth's still current *Portnoy's Complaint*, our literature has lent its traditional dignity to the idea that

American women alternate a diet of husbands with a diet of sons.

Nor is it solely on the ground of her inordinate appetites that the American mother is chivied and mocked: If she cannot be blamed for devouring her young, she is blamed for rejecting them. For some fifty years now, it has been impossible for a woman, especially a mother, to be anything but wrong in our culture; and the more supposedly enlightened her community, the more varied and virulent the attacks, to the point where one often has the impression that the prestige of our best and most progressive private schools is built on the humiliations of young mothers. Moreover, this pernicious assault on women's minds and spirits comes not alone from men. Perhaps even more of the time, it comes from other women.

Any adequate statement of woman's inhumanity to woman might perhaps suggest that what eventually is wrong with women is that there are other women in the world, and that women are to be condemned out of hand for their betrayals, overt and covert, of their own sex. But such harsh judgments of women minimize the range and subtlety of the difficulties by which they are beset. It may not be very edifying to contemplate the spectacle of women acceding in whatever is the form that the disparagement of their own sex may at the moment be taking just so that men will be reassured that they deserve the status conferred upon them by their superior biological endowment, but if it is on a man's sexual confidence that a woman's sexual and maternal satisfactions depend, and if, too, the male in our society is willing to pay for his biological advantage by assuming the financial support of his wife and family, it is more than understandable, it is plainest reason, that a woman should place the male interest, whether real or only fancied, above that of other women.

In particular it is understandable that women should come to feel that they are not defeated but fulfilled in accepting the passivity that is implied by acknowledging man's

primary sexual-social role. For living by one's deference to
the needs of those one loves is one of the pleasanter modes
of existence—as well as, I might add, one of the most taxing.
It is a grave fault of modern culture that it trains us in the
belief that whatever defers to others is an *in*action and
therefore of only secondary social value.

And yet, even while we record the appeal on behalf of
passivity, the question presses upon us whether our female-
ists, who stress their satisfaction in devoting their lives to
being good wives and mothers, would settle for this domestication of their capacities if they lived in a society where
different requirements were made of women than are made
in our culture. We are told that the women in the Israeli
kibbutzim who serve side by side with their men in the army
and in the fields and who give up the larger part of the
rearing of their children to communal nurseries show no
sign of being unfulfilled as women. Nor, apparently, are
their men castrated by this sexual equality. It would also
seem clear from Solzhenitsyn's remarkable novel *Cancer
Ward* that, although a woman surgeon in the Soviet Union
may return from a grueling day in the cancer hospital and,
like working wives everywhere in our servantless world, still
accept it as her job to do the marketing, cooking, cleaning,
and laundry, it is not in her home and family but in her
"real" work, her man's work if you will, that she invests her
pride of being, including her peculiarly feminine pride of
being. It is undoubtedly one of the significant revelations of
this book that in a situation where the women carry equal
responsibilities with men it is still the men who fill the top
hospital posts; but no less fascinating is its revelation of the
many wholly unself-conscious ways in which the women
physicians manage to irradiate their grim hospital routines
with a sexually distinguishing gentleness and delicacy. From
evidences like these I think we must conclude that women
are considerably more flexible in the matter of how they
can derive their fulfillment than most American women are
yet prepared to recognize, and that it is perhaps only be-

cause our culture prefers that its women find their best satisfaction in the activities of home and family that the women themselves obediently discover it there.

In other words, we are all of us, men and women both, the creatures of culture: We do and feel what our societies want us to do and feel, and the demands that they put upon us are not always either very consistent or very precisely correlated with biology. In wartime, for instance, when men are away and women not only take jobs in factories and on farms but make all the financial and practical decisions usually made by the male head of the family, no one thinks of accusing them of conduct unbecoming a woman. Or if a woman is forced through widowhood to earn her own living, no one is moved to put a brake on her competitiveness with men; she is thought a castrating woman only if she now switches the dependence she once had on her husband to her grown children.

And in a similar reversal of values, I can imagine a moment—and perhaps a not very distant moment—when the conserving instinct of women will become the most active force (and I emphasize the word "active") in the continuing life of society. I have in mind the active role that women may soon be called upon to play in rescuing the modern world from pollution; and when I say called upon, I mean called upon not by men but by themselves, by their own intelligence and appreciation of the extent of the emergency. Since so far it seems to be impossible for men to mobilize the energies they use for the conquest of other planets for the preservation of life on Earth, women may well have to take over the job. This is one kind of activity in culture, one form of competitiveness beyond the limits of home and family, in which the female sex would surely excel: the competition to perpetuate life. It is a program to which Women's Liberation could, and should, rally all women.

But when I say that women are the creatures of culture, while I obviously mean the prevailing culture, I do not necessarily mean only the dominant culture of the society. It may well be that among those who most dramatically dissent from our dominant culture, and in particular among the young, there are being forged attitudes that will importantly alter the relation of the sexes in the dominant culture of the future.

I suppose it is natural enough that in the matter of renovating the relations of men and women it is on the score of women's professional and legal rights that the voice of contemporary protest is making itself most readily heard. This is perhaps the area in which men are finally the least challenged; it is, of course, the area that is sanctioned by the historical efforts on behalf of sexual equality. It is nevertheless possible, I think, that the cause of women's professional rights—the demand that women receive equal pay for equal work and similar advancement for similar merit—may be becoming our newest middle-class liberal ritualism, to be embraced as a way of avoiding the need to look more closely at less crude but more troubling manifestations of the lack of parity between the sexes. I myself happen to think, for instance, that, although it will indeed be a great day for women when they are appointed to full professorships at our leading universities on the same basis as men, it will be an even greater day for women when right in their own living rooms they are given as much serious attention and credence as men now receive when they pass judgment, especially adverse judgment, on an idea or a person.

It is not, however, the overt agitations on behalf of women that I actually have in mind when I speculate upon the possible effect our present-day dissent may eventually have upon the dominant culture. I am not closely enough acquainted with the dissident young to know exactly what decorousnesses, rules, and formalities pertain to their sexual relations, or what constitute their criteria of sexual worth and loyalty. What is nevertheless apparent even at my distance is the pervasive devaluation of those appurtenances of masculinity and femininity that our culture—by which I chiefly mean our competitive economy—sanctified for an earlier generation. I was myself of a generation in which any deviation from the specifications for female charm, as set down by Madison Avenue and the movies, was thought seriously to reduce a girl's sexual bargaining power. While intellectually we knew that the models by which we presumably were judged and by which we judged ourselves were the exceptions in any race of mortals, we suffered the private anguishes of living under the sexual dictates not of nature but of commerce. One recalls the father in Dostoevski's *The Brothers Karamazov* who said there was no such thing as an ugly woman: The possibility that an opinion like this would one day infiltrate large sections of our society was beyond our wildest dreams, strained as we were by the demands for an ideal femininity put upon us by advertising and by Hollywood. This strain would happily seem to be gone, having disappeared in the radical effort to disavow the dominant capitalist culture. And as a woman, even though not a revolutionary, I can hope it is gone forever.

And gone—or going—with it, through the same effort, is the social-sexual differentiation between men and women in terms of dress and hairstyle. While I confess to having no love for the shared slovenliness of so many young men and women, since I see in it a depreciation of their pride in themselves as persons, I welcome the unisexual appearance of the sexes if only for its criticism of a culture in which sexually differentiated styles of hair and dress, designed not by God but by man, were treated as if they were biological actualities. As I see it, or at least as I hope it, whatever reduces the false separations between men and women is bound to reduce their suspicions and hostilities, and thus permit them a fuller expression of their human potentiality. Free of the cultural detritus of our sexual differences, perhaps we can come to a sounder and happier knowledge of our distinctive maleness and femaleness than is now permitted us.

THE WORKING MOTHER'S CRISES [5]

After the morning rush, eight hours at the office, the freeway, fixing dinner, putting the children to bath and bed, running a load of clothes in the washer, the working mother thinks about child care as she does dishes at 10:30 P.M.

She gives it lots of thought because she knows that it costs a lot for baby sitters or nursery schools. It costs a lot to feed and clothe everyone. And she's working for a paycheck: nine out of ten women work for monetary reasons. . . .

And she isn't always satisfied with the care the children get. It frustrates her: It's part of living, like taxes going up and the groceries costing more and the bad air.

But it's not like the roof leaking when it rains. It's not like the pilot going out on the gas dryer. It's not like the wallpaper order coming in orange flowers instead of red. It's not like the car battery going dead.

Child Needs Repairs

These things can be repaired or replaced.

But a child. That's different. He gets the child care his parents provide him—what's available at what they can afford. And most of the time it isn't good enough. So the child needs repairs. But can you repair a child?

Research shows that the first three years of a child's life largely determine his future.

And yet, seemingly, when their children need them most, millions of mothers are deserting the cradle to rock the labor force.

Since just before World War II, the number of working women (now thirty million) has more than doubled, but the number of working mothers has increased almost eightfold.

The trend is expected to continue. Projections for 1985 from the United States Department of Labor indicate that 6.6 million mothers ages twenty to forty-four with children

[5] From article by Mary Lou Loper, staff writer. Los Angeles *Times*. p 1. Ap. 18, '71. Copyright, 1971, Los Angeles *Times*. Reprinted by permission.

under age five will be in the labor force. This will represent a 32 percent increase between 1975 and 1985.

In California, there are now 1.035 million working mothers with children eighteen years or less, and 388,125 with children under six years.

"Leftover" Care

For years, authorities have been suggesting that children of working mothers are second-class citizens relegated to "leftover" care. Too many, says a HEW [United States Department of Health, Education, and Welfare] Department of Labor survey, "receive questionable and inadequate care."

Authorities, however, are in agreement that steps must be taken to provide better care. What "better care" is and whether working mothers can afford it is a point of dispute.

Nevertheless, the boom is on.

Business, labor, students, government, psychiatrists, social workers, welfare workers, fathers, volunteers, Women's Lib have talked about child care. Industry has viewed it (though cautiously) in terms of providing a stable work force. New careerists have praised it in terms of potential new jobs.

Builders are including day-care centers in new housing developments as an enticement to sell homes and condominiums. Franchise outfits are competing in day care for profit and there are visions of Kentucky Fried Children.

Two Presidents have advocated child care.

President Johnson in a 1967 message to Congress said:

Ignorance, ill health, personality disorder—these are disabilities often contracted in childhood: afflictions which linger to cripple the man and damage the next generation. Our nation must rid itself of this bitter inheritance. Our goal must be clear—to give every child the chance to fulfill his promise.

President Nixon echoed the opinion in his August 1969 message to Congress. He asked for "a national commitment to provide all American children an opportunity for healthful and stimulating development during the first five years of life . . ."

Little, however, has been done to help solve the problem of child care for or by the bulk of American working mothers. Various bills being introduced in Congress may turn the tide.

There is a notion that, like a car, if we develop an expensive child-care model which works, it may be put on an assembly line and mass-produced, turning out smooth-running children who perform well in their school years.

Mrs. Richard M. Lansburgh, a member of the board of directors of the Day Care and Development Council of America and its former president, believes that "America needs a coordinated network of child-care and development services for children of . . . [all ages] and that quality child-care services "are a right of every child of every parent of every community."

Such a venture would cost at least $9 billion annually, it is estimated.

However, high costs of child care already are turning working mothers gray. Furthermore, good child care often isn't there, even when the conscientious mother seeks it and can pay the asking price.

Who are these some twelve million working mothers who put themselves on a treadmill?

How old are these working mothers? Median age is thirty-seven (median age of all women workers is thirty-nine).

How married? Eighty-four percent have a husband present in the home.

How affluent? One of every twelve has a husband with an income less than $3,000; far more mothers work outside the home when their husbands' incomes are low.

The Department of Labor survey also showed that a mother's decision to work part time is influenced by the ages of her children; the proportion who work full time year-round is lowest among those with children less than three years; a woman is more apt to work if she has a female relative in her home or close by.

What Price Care?

And how do mothers care for their children and how much do they pay?

The most recent comprehensive national survey of child-care arrangements (conducted by the HEW's Children's Bureau and the Women's Bureau, United States Department of Labor, disclosed that nearly half of children of working mothers are cared for in their own homes while the mother works.

Child care in someone else's home (family day-care) was provided for 16 percent. Another 13 percent were looked after by the mother while she worked; 15 percent had mothers who worked only during the children's school hours and required no special arrangements.

Another 3 percent were cared for in day-care centers, nursery schools or other group facilities. (Among children under six, however, 6 percent were cared for in groups.) And nearly one million children (8 percent) looked after themselves while their mothers worked.

Results showed that of women making payment for child care, 24 percent paid less than $5 a week per child; 40 percent, $5-$9 a week; 32 percent, $10-$19, and 4 percent, $20 or more. These costs should be approximately doubled per mother since the mothers surveyed had an average of two children each.

Group day-care, the survey said, was among the most costly of arrangements.

Nationally, group day-care in licensed centers is available for only 640,000 children, though it is estimated that several million need the service.

The topic, high costs of child care, raises additional important points:

    1. There are no guarantees that if women made higher salaries they would apply them to better child care.

    2. There are no guarantees that if lower-cost child-care in centers were available to middle-class mothers they would use it.

Some women always will prefer to keep their young at home, cared for maybe, by a grandmother whose ideas may smell of lavender, but who is grandmother and knit to the family.

Nevertheless, perhaps, as a society, we have tended to look with romantic bias on each home "sweet home," while inside those four walls children were not always receiving the best, even the good.

Child care, yet, has far to go.

RAISING A BRIGHT AND HAPPY CHILD [6]

Blond, three-year-old Kim works diligently on a puzzle in her nursery school classroom. When the teacher says she is going to serve juice and cookies, Kim murmurs to herself, "I like apple juice best." Slipping the last piece of the puzzle into place, she smiles happily over the accomplishment. When her teacher calls "Cleanup time," Kim obediently puts the puzzle back in its correct place.

Tommy, also three, behaves very differently. When he works on a puzzle he often stops halfway and scatters the pieces. Unable to find a toy that holds his interest for more than a few minutes, he tends to wander aimlessly around the classroom. Unlike Kim, who gets along well with other children even though she usually gets her own way ("Kim just seems to know when to lead and when to follow," says her

[6] Article by free-lance writer Myrna Blyth. *Woman's Day*. p 46-7. My. '71. Reprinted by permission of Curtis Brown, Ltd. Copyright © 1971 by Fawcett Publications, Inc.

teacher), Tommy throws temper tantrums or dissolves into helpless tears when thwarted.

Although they have similar middle-class backgrounds, these two children have obviously reached vastly different levels of intellectual competence and emotional maturity. What is the reason for so many differences at such an early age? No one answer is conclusive. Inherited abilities and many varied environmental factors contribute to the special development of every child. Research studies indicate, however, that the way a mother treats her child during the second and third year of life is of vital importance. In fact, some psychologists at Harvard are increasingly sure that the environmental factor with the greatest effect on a preschool child's level of development is the quality of mothering he receives.

Dr. Burton L. White, a father of four and the director of Harvard's Pre-School Project, describes his work testing and studying very young children as "the greatest job in the world. In the last five years," he adds, "more and more people have become convinced of the importance of education before the age of six. And it's only in the past two or three years that research has really concentrated on children under three."

This attention to *pre*-preschool education began when educators learned that children from deprived homes are often far behind many of their more affluent classmates by the time they enter school. Middle-class children often develop more skills and abilities during the first years of life— long before formal schooling begins. How they acquire this important extra knowledge is what Dr. White and other researchers are focusing on.

"When all this information about deprived youngsters first came out," explains Dr. White, "a lot of people said they knew how to help these children improve their abilities. Well, we took a different approach. We said we were not sure how to cope with the problem and would try to learn from what already existed. We set out to find a six-year-old everyone agreed was doing wonderfully well, and then discover what made him such a superior child. We wanted to learn what certain families were doing *right!*"

Dr. White and a dozen fellow researchers visited nursery schools, kindergartens and Project Head Start centers in the greater Boston area. The outstanding three- to six-year-olds they found became known as their "A" group, while others, who appeared to be healthy but didn't seem to cope very well from day to day, comprised their "C" group. Unlike most recent studies, this one did not concentrate on deprived children. "We didn't have any really impoverished families or any upper-upper-class children," admits Dr. Robert LaCrosse, one of the Project's researchers. "But then," he adds puckishly, "I've never seen a study on how to raise a Rockefeller or a Rothschild."

Dr. White and his colleagues watched and compared these "A" and "C" children for nearly a year and made a startling discovery: their three-year-old "A" children were doing far better—both intellectually and socially—than their six-year-old "C" children. What could an "A" child do that made him so special? . . . For one thing, Dr. White explains, an "A" child could "dual focus"—he could, like Kim, make a pertinent remark on one subject while working on something else. The "A" child also exhibited an ability to anticipate consequences to an unusual degree. When another child picked up a pitcher of water with one hand, for instance, Jimmy shouted: "Watch it! Use both hands! You're going to spill it all over the floor." In addition, the "A" child can plan and carry out multistep activity. One little girl who spilled paint on her dress told her nursery school teacher solemnly: "You go home. You get me another dress. You bring it here. I'll put it on."

As Dr. White is quick to point out, he and his colleagues were not just testing IQs, but looking for all-around competence. They sought preschoolers with outstanding social abilities as well as intellectual skills. "These children can almost 'con' adults into giving them what they want," he says. "They know how to use adults as a resource." Also, interestingly, they spend a lot of time playing "grown-up," and indicating a desire to achieve. To illustrate, Dr. White cites one three-year-old who rushed about officiously declaring, "I'm Bob Important."

Since these exceptional three-year-olds obviously developed their abilities *before* nursery school, Dr. White's project shifted its sights downward and began to study children between the ages of one and three in their natural habitat—right at home. (They didn't study babies less than a year old because most infants seem to react to psychological tests in much the same way. The reason, according to some psychologists, is that most normal mothers do a satisfactory job of caring for their infants in the first year. Other authorities disagree, saying differences are formed in the earliest months of a baby's life, but they haven't, as yet, found adequate tests to reveal them.)

Armed with tape recorders and notebooks, Dr. White and the other researchers examined the behavior of mothers and young children in the manner of anthropologists tracing the customs of a primitive tribe. Some concentrated on noting exactly what toddlers do all day, while others observed the mothers. At first they had to contend with what they called the "girdles on" and "living room spotless" syndrome. "You arrive at eight thirty and are greeted by a tidy house and mother wearing basic black with pearls and a girdle," recalls one researcher. "We knew we were successful," she continued, "when we arrived on a subsequent visit and found the beds unmade, Mother in a housecoat and the kitchen in chaos."

After a year and a half, Dr. White and his staff began putting observations together and discovered an intriguing pattern. They could identify at least five distinct types of mothers. The first type, the woman who usually produces an exceptional child, became known as the Supermother. She educates her child constantly, but not in any formal or rigid manner. According to Dr. White, she teaches casually, as part of her daily routine, and enjoys and accepts her child at his level of development. She does not try to teach her two-year-old to read, but she may show him how to drop wooden shapes in the correct holes in a drop-box.

Part of this mother's success stems from the fact that she reads, sings songs, and does a lot of talking to her child. While walking with a toddler she may say: "That's a big red truck. It's a moving truck. I guess new people are moving in there." She takes one idea, elaborates on it, adds bits of relevant information. These short but frequent episodes help to increase the toddler's vocabulary and general fund of knowledge.

In addition, she plays with her children. "I'm a nurse," says three-year-old Lisa.

"Will you bandage my hand?" her mother responds promptly. "That's what nurses do—bandage hands, give injections, help the doctor." This mother tries to reward her child's achievements, too. When the baby puts the right lid back on the saucepan, she applauds.

Type two, referred to as the Almost Mother, tries but doesn't reach the same high standards. Although she enjoys and accepts her child, too, she often has trouble understanding or satisfying his needs—especially before he can talk. During the toddler stage, she misses many chances to teach. On a walk she may say, "See the truck," but that's as far as it goes. She seems to lack the capacity for making spontaneous associations that heighten a child's interests.

The third type of mother, one who is beaten down by the difficult circumstances of her life, was called the Overwhelmed Mother. Her children spend a great deal of their time in aimless, unmonitored behavior. "The overwhelmed mother may have eight kids and only thirty dollars a week for food," says one project researcher, "but middle-class mothers can be overwhelmed, too." Dr. White believes that children born too close together can overtax even a very talented woman. "One woman did a great job with her two girls, now three and four, but she also has a vigorous, adventurous eighteen-month-old boy. Her husband likes the house kept very neat, too." Dr. White shakes his head in sympathy. He now believes that his own four children, two girls ten and eight, and two boys seven and four, may have been too closely spaced.

The last two types, called the Smothering Mother and the Zoo-keeper Mother, are directly opposite in behavior. The Smothering Mother pushes her child to achieve. As one researcher put it, "she's preparing him for Harvard at the age of two." She is so responsive to his every little need that he rarely has an opportunity to take the initiative or to express himself. This mother spends hour after hour drilling her child on how to perform and gets some positive results for her efforts. Her child is apt to have high intellectual skills but he may also be whiny, clingy and socially immature.

The Zoo-keeper Mother, on the other hand, spends too little time with her child. She is too involved in her own social life or in keeping to a rigid housekeeping schedule to find time to talk to or play with her toddler. In the words of one researcher, "she seems to be waiting for him to be old enough to play golf or bridge." Her child is likely to be apathetic and to spend much of his time alone—often in an immaculate crib in an expensively furnished nursery filled with the latest toys.

As Dr. White and his colleagues are quick to point out, many mothers do not fit neatly into any of these categories. The project's use of these classifications is intended only to help explain different maternal styles and how they affect a child's ability. Overall, Dr. White's study seems to suggest that a mother is not only her child's first teacher; she may be his most important one as well.

Other current studies confirm the effectiveness of a mother as educator during the earliest learning years. One program, in fact, made use of this concept in order to raise the IQs of a group of two- and three-year-olds in a Long Island housing project. Dr. Phyllis Levenstein, head of the Verbal Interaction Project's Mother-Child Home Program, sent toy demonstrators into homes to show mothers how to use specially selected books and toys. Then, the demonstrators encouraged the mothers to interact with their children. The toys served mainly as a focus for mother and child to talk about and play with together. After several years, the program's results are impressive and gratifying. The first group of children had an IQ rise of seventeen points, while some have made leaps of as much as forty points.

Dr. Earl S. Schaefer, Chief of the Early Child Care Research Center at the National Institute of Mental Health, also believes that education begins at home. He points to studies suggesting that children's IQs may rise and their abilities increase after being tested and retested over a period of months. Do children learn from the tests? No, thinks Dr. Schaefer, but their mothers probably do. After watching their children being tested, some mothers may begin instructing their children so they can do better on their next test. Thanks to the mothers' efforts, the children often do.

Obviously, then, the responsibility for a child's earliest learning rests on his mother's already overburdened shoulders. How does she begin? The first step, say the experts, is often just a matter of following her own natural mothering instincts. When a mother ministers to a child as soon as he cries, she leads him to believe he can affect his world. And, in the words of one researcher, "a child needs this confidence in order to learn."

The mother who claims she doesn't believe in "spoiling" and never picks up her wailing infant may think she is giving her baby "character," but she's probably doing just the opposite. Her child will stop crying when the crying has no effect, but his silence doesn't indicate self-reliance—just helplessness. The mother who says, "He never gives me any trouble," about her overly docile toddler may later regret the many problems that lie ahead for such a stifled child.

The positive relationship between mother and child that is so important to learning is developed in thousands of little ways. The experts say it begins when you talk to your baby

—and not just at playtime, either. When you are feeding, bathing or changing an infant, coo a bit, sing to him, tell him what a joy and wonder he is. The baby may not understand what you're saying, but he'll learn that language makes him feel happy—so happy that he'll try to "talk" himself. Psychologists also recommend taking time out to involve your baby in reciprocal games—peek-a-boo, for instance. Give him stimulating objects to look at and reach for, and show him how they move or make pleasing sounds when touched. By making his life as interesting as possible, you encourage him to learn.

As every mother knows, a baby changes dramatically at around twelve or fifteen months. The infant who was content to spend much of the day in crib or playpen becomes an aggressive toddler. As he learns to use his legs, he also discovers what marvelous instruments his hands are. He picks a can off the food shelf, tries to taste it, sniff it, roll it. Finally he abandons it in the middle of the floor and goes off to wreak havoc by pulling the dog's tail or knocking over the tower of bricks his four-year-old brother has carefully constructed. "You have to watch him every single minute," is the despairing wail of the toddler's exhausted mother.

"This is a very difficult time," agrees Dr. White, "A small child roaming about puts a great deal of extra stress on the family." A mother who could cope easily and successfully with her malleable infant may be unable to manage her adventurous toddler. "At this point," says one Harvard researcher, "some good first-year mothers become Almost Mothers." The Harvard team found, however, that the exceptional mother is able to recognize and respond to her child's new state of growth. She "child-proofs" her home—puts away fragile table ornaments and locks the medicine and household cleaners out of her toddler's eager reach—then lets her child explore.

This mother is aware that her awkward child is trying to master the skills of a civilized human being. Tommy holds his cup in his two hands, tilts it, spills his milk down his bib. He puts his spoon in his cereal, tries to find his mouth, smears his chin instead, Tommy's mother may groan inwardly but she keeps smiling as she wipes up the mess. She knows that practice alone can give Tommy the dexterity he needs in order to feed himself neatly and independently.

A good mother also helps her child develop what psychologists call eye-hand coordination. She might cut a slot in the top of a jar and encourage her toddler to drop colored buttons through the slot. Or perhaps she'll make a stroke with a crayon and then ask him to imitate what she's drawn. Surprisingly, he can! The toddler can also learn to sort objects of a similar shape, color or texture and to fit together the pieces of a very simple puzzle. As his hands become more skillful, he concentrates longer on an activity, learns to complete a task, and gains a beneficial feeling of accomplishment.

Obviously, the mother who lets her child scatter clothespins, sort pots and pans on the kitchen floor and pour water from one container to another lets herself in for annoying extra work. Even the most dedicated parent has frustrating moments. Recalling his son's toddler years, Dr. White confesses: "One day he managed to destroy parts of a very nice car with a hammer. I know he didn't do it maliciously but . . ." He shakes his head and looks, for an instant, more like a slightly befuddled father than an all-knowing child psychologist.

In these early years, a child embarks on a phenomenal intellectual achievement: learning to talk. "Doggie," cries the thirteen-month-old chasing the neighborhood poodle. "See the doggie," shouts an excited seventeen-month-old who has, in just four months, made a giant leap forward by learning how to put words together. A child without adequate language facility is severely handicapped. At least half of every IQ test is really the test of language ability. No matter how much innate potential a child may have, he will never be able to express it without a good vocabulary.

The ability to speak, read and write effectively is developed step by step, but it all begins with the toddler learning how to talk. Thus, a mother's most important educational role may be that of first language teacher for her child. Ideally, she teaches continually but casually. Finding a caterpillar in the yard, she says, "Look, Billy, a caterpillar. Feel how soft it is." Billy answers, "Caterpillar," as he studies the creature with interest. When mother straps Billy into his car seat she says, "We're going to the supermarket to buy some milk and eggs." As they pull into the parking lot, Billy realizes that the place where Mommy buys her cookies is called the supermarket. The next time he's strapped in, he declares, "Supermarket! Let's go!"

Every mother talks to her child, of course, but in varying degrees. Studies show that some ghetto mothers, for instance occasionally issue commands but rarely have give-and-take conversations with their young children. Dr. White's project revealed that some affluent mothers do not talk much either. One New York City pediatrician told me of seeing many three-year-olds "who speak with West Indian or French or Scottish accents although they were all born here. Their mothers never have time to talk to them; only the maids do!"

In contrast, the superior mother uses language to teach important concepts to her youngsters. Passing a store window, she may say, "That dress is blue. Your coat is blue, too. I like blue," making her little girl aware of colors and their names. She teaches about size ("What a big house. It's bigger than our house!") and about shape ("The ball is round and the block is square. Can you show me something else that's round?").

Though Mother plays a starring role in the drama of a child's development, his father, brothers and sisters and grandparents have leading parts, too. In fact, Dr. Earl Schaefer believes that the father's importance is often ignored with less-than-happy results. He cites a study in which very alienated youngsters described their mothers as "hostile and overinvolved," while their fathers were seen as "distant, ignoring, very detached." Obviously, as Dr. Schaefer put it, "the healthy child needs both a mother and a father who is active and involved in his upbringing from the start."

On a practical level, Dr. Phyllis Levenstein notes that a two-year-old in her program "was tutored" very successfully by his father and the rest of his family after his mother became ill. By the age of four this child's IQ had risen from a below-average 86 to a superior 129. Many mothers believe second and third children are "quicker" simply because their older brothers and sisters enjoy teaching and seem to know instinctively how much the younger child can learn. One seven-year-old who taught his four-year-old sister to read was not very impressed by her ability or his own skill. "I just showed her a few times," he explained casually to his amazed, delighted parents.

Intellectual skills are, of course, only one part of a child's development. Dr. White's superior three-year-olds are special because they are emotionally mature as well. Raising a self-reliant, relatively fearless and happy child is just as much an accomplishment as raising a clever one. "Oddly enough," Dr. White says, "we found the best mothers were not all that child-oriented. The exceptional mother seems to have enough personal security to stop her child from doing what she doesn't like. She can say no, and she does say no, and she doesn't feel guilty about saying it."

In contrast, the Smothering Mother caters too much to her child and makes him overly dependent; the Zoo-keeper Mother achieves the same result by the opposite route. The ideal mother gives her child the freedom to explore but not to create chaos. She says yes often enough—"Yes, I'll read you a story"; "Yes, I'll help you with your puzzle"—so she can say no when necessary with absolute firmness. By her actions, says Dr. White, "she gives her child a realistic understanding of the world."

The value of an education has long been known, but now we know that learning begins long before a child enters school. And if his earliest education is deficient he may never be able to make up the loss. Although youngsters learn throughout childhood—and hopefully, throughout their lives —a child never learns as quickly or as much as does in his first five years.

The mother of small children is often harried, over-worked and even bored by her tiring routine. But when she realizes the important effect she has on her children at this time, it seems like a small price to pay. "The beginning is the most important part of the work," Plato wrote. The woman who believes this and acts upon her belief is already on her way to raising an exceptional child.

CHILDREN AND THEIR FAMILIES [7]

With so many ills of our society being challenged by the young—racial injustice, unnecessary poverty, pollution, imperialism—it's not surprising that all aspects of family life are up for sharp questioning and experimentation. The former sentimental ideal of a large family of children is now considered irresponsible. Couples are living together outside marriage more openly. Young people are experimenting with communes. Untraditional roles for women and men—in the family and at work outside—are being discussed seriously, as are new ways for bringing up children.

Women are demanding the same opportunity as men to get into the challenging and prestigious jobs, equal pay for similar work, equal consideration for promotion—matters in which they have been almost universally cheated.

Women are expressing vigorous resentment at the exploitation of themselves as characterless sexual objects—in advertising, girlie magazines, songs, jokes, and in life itself.

They resent the lordly attitude of the men who blandly assume the superiority of their sex or who noisily assert it

[7] From *Decent and Indecent: Our Personal and Political Behavior*, by Benjamin Spock, M.D. rev. ed. Fawcett. '71. Reprinted by permission of the McCall Publishing Company. © 1969, 1970, 1971 by James M. Houston, Trustee, under an Irrevocable Trust Dated October 6, 1966, between Benjamin M. Spock of Cleveland, Ohio, Donor, and James M. Houston of Pittsburgh, Pennsylvania, Trustee.

or who show obvious prejudice about which they are quite unconscious.

Most basically they protest against being relegated automatically to an inferior status—occupationally and domestically—in which vital decisions are made for them by male employers and relatives, or by the society as a whole, often without their even being consulted. To put it positively, they want to be in charge of their lives and to have an equal voice and equal consideration in all home and job matters. Through these means they seek not merely justice for themselves but the opportunity to share in the making of a better life for the family, the community, and the world.

To provide mothers an equal access to jobs, they suggest various alternatives: nurseries provided by the state for the all-day (or even twenty-four-hour) care of children from birth until they can attend publicly supported nursery schools at three years; staggered work hours for the father and mother, so that one parent can always be at home; a number of families living together in a group or commune so that child care can be shared or so that parents who prefer to stay at home can care for the children while others go out to work.

It's proposed that mothers be no more restricted to the home by housework and child care than fathers, and that men, in any case, do 50 percent of this work; that if one partner is to stay permanently at home, it could just as appropriately be the father.

Women who have not made up their minds yet are joining various groups that are springing up throughout the country, first to clarify what their situations and their feelings are in a man-dominated society and then to discuss alternatives. Many men, mostly young ones, have already been won over to the cause.

The present trend of more and more women going to work outside the home will continue, I believe—either because they need the money, want to pursue a career, simply desire to be useful, crave company, or because of some combination of these. They will be able to find the time for jobs because among other reasons, many of them will have had their last child by the age of twenty-five.

I myself hope, though, that we never come to the day when it is assumed that an outside job is an obligation (aside from financial necessity), or is more creative or gives greater fulfillment than the care of children and the home —for women or men.

It may turn out in the long run, if the work week is progressively shortened and if wage and prestige differentials are minimized, that most men and women will think of their gratifications as coming primarily from home and from various artistic, intellectual, humanitarian and recreational activities. Then the satisfactions from what we now call employment may be considered less vital—at least in those industrial jobs which prove difficult for technical reasons (e.g. the assembly line) to endow with any creativity or meaning.

Parents' Influence on the Child

In the experimentation with new roles for fathers and mothers, what has been learned in this century about the emotional needs of young children should be taken into account.

The personality of a child is extremely impressionable in his first three years. He is being constantly molded by his parents or by the substitute who spends the greatest amount of time with him. Whether the child becomes a trusting or a suspicious person will be determined by whether his parents are responsive in meeting his needs and steady in their mood or are disturbingly unpredictable. Whether he will be loving or cool for the rest of his life will depend on their level of warmth. One person acts toward children as if they were basically "bad," always doubting them, scolding them. Another trustingly assumes that at bottom they are good. Children become what they are expected to be. A parent with more than average hostility or irritability finds a dozen excuses every hour of the day for venting it—openly or subtly—on the child, and the child's character acquires a corresponding hostility. There are lots of people who have the itch to dominate children and others who want to keep them dependent or babyish; they can succeed.

Good parents don't merely meet the physical needs of their baby. They take a great and special delight in him. They tell him he's the most appealing baby in the world and he shows he appreciates their confidence and warmth. They have a drive to foster all aspects of his development. They try from birth to get a smile out of him and they use baby talk (for his first eighteen months only) to teach him a few understandable words. They teach him peek-a-boo, play him his favorite records, and point out the pictures in his books. These aren't merely intellectual teaching exercises. They are expressions of an intense emotional relationship. That is why a loved baby keeps surging ahead— intellectually, socially, emotionally—and an unappreciated baby keeps getting slowed down along the way.

The influence that makes children grow up to become the people who have the extra motivation to go to college or to carry on an occupation that's above the humdrum level is having lived with, felt cherished by, wanting to be like parents who had such aspirations—whether or not the parents were able to carry them out. And we've learned from psychoanalytic studies that the influence which makes a very few individuals become extraordinarily productive or creative is, most often, the inspiration they received from a strong relationship with a mother who had especially high aspirations.

There are few parent substitutes (whether a relation or a hired person) who have the time or impulse to lavish all these expressions of love and hope, though there are a few.

If a child develops a real dependence on a substitute who takes over most of his care and if the substitute then leaves him, the deprivation will be deep and will have long-lasting effects. If he is repeatedly left by a succession of caretakers, he may develop, as a defense against future such desertions, a fundamental reluctance to love deeply anyone else again.

I should interject that of course I don't mean that parents have to worry about the perfection of character of everyone who has regular contact with their child. It is good for him to be acquainted with a variety of people: relatives, neighbors of all ages, storekeepers. They will enrich his personality. What I've been pointing out is the influence of the person who takes over the mother's and father's place in the sense of being with the child most of his waking hours, the one to whom he comes to turn for comfort and security. The influence is heightened, unfortunately, if the substitute is possessive or domineering or mean; and also if the parents' interest in their child is shallow.

I'd suggest as a very rough guide that in the first three years of life a child should be cared for at least two thirds of his waking hours by his parents, grandparents, or other close relatives in whom the parents have great confidence —in the sense that they are happy to have this relative shaping the child's personality. If they are to hire someone for most of the waking hours, they should make sure— over a period of weeks and months—that this person has a character and attitude that thoroughly suits them and will stick with the job for years. If the child is to be left in another person's home, there should not be more than three children under six years there.

If the mother is to take the larger part of the care of the child under three years, she could still go to work for, say two or three half-days a week, more if it is evening work when the father would be at home. By the time the child is in nursery school, the mother could expand her work schedule to five half-days and, when he is in elementary school, to five days of work up to 3:00 P.M.

The staggering of working hours of father and mother will provide full security and stimulation for the child. But matching schedules are hard to arrange. And with the traditional eight-hour work day this method separates the parents severely. It should work better as automation gradually reduces the work day.

A father could take all-day care of his child while the mother works full time if the parents agree that this is the best solution. If neither parent is ready to take time out from a career to care for a child for a few years, and if there is no other fond relative available, I'd advise them not to have a child. To be sure, if they truly yearn for a child, they may be able to find someone to give him loving and stable care; but the search for a good parent substitute becomes more difficult each year.

Certainly, if either parent dislikes or is bored by children they should not have any. For their children would have serious emotional problems.

I believe the government should pay a basic salary to the mother or father who stays at home to care for young children, on the basis that this is a good investment. If the mother had started on a career before her pregnancy and is to be the major caretaker, her employer should be legally required to provide her with part-time work and to maintain her full seniority during her child's early years.

If communes become at all prevalent, the crucial question for parents both of whom want an outside job is whether the other person who will take the major care of their baby is one whom they know they can trust, who will stay in the commune and who will continue to care for their child. I believe that a small child should have consistent care from the same person for at least half his waking hours.

What about state-supported nurseries from birth, the solution so often proposed today?

Most of the day nurseries that have existed for the last hundred years in the United States, to care for the babies and children of mothers who were compelled to work (usually, before the days of welfare payments, because they had been widowed or deserted), have had multiple defects: inadequate, untrained staff, babies lying in their cribs, isolated and deserted; and many of the mothers who took them home at night so demoralized by their bitter life experiences that they could not provide sufficient affection or attention either. These deprived children made poor records in school and in life, and nurseries got a bad reputation.

The nurseries for children of working mothers in the Soviet Union and in the kibbutzim in Israel (the agricultural communities in which both parents work and the children are cared for, except for evenings with the parents, in nurseries and boarding schools) have been much more satisfactory than American day nurseries of the past. They have been amply staffed with selected, trained attendants. But the results in the crucial first three years have not yet been *proved* ideal enough to overcome the skepticism of a professional person like myself who has high aspirations for his children.

The older generation of intellectual, idealistic Jews from Europe who settled in Israel between World Wars I and II are very proud of their sons and daughters who were raised in the kibbutzim and whom they consider ideal citizens as well as ideal soldiers. "But," an older person comments wistfully, "the only trouble is that they aren't Jews." He is not referring to religious belief. He means that the group upbringing has produced a noticeably different personality type. Whereas the older settler from Europe tended to be a philosophical, imaginative, sociable person with strong emotional ties to his relatives, his son or grandson is more apt to become a highly practical, matter-of-fact, and duty-bound citizen, often hard to get to know. I'm not saying that one type is better than another, only that they are different.

School achievement test scores of children raised in the kibbutzim tend to be concentrated in the middle zone, compared to children raised in their homes of whom an appreciable proportion are either in the high or the low zones, depending on the quality of the home atmosphere. So group rearing (of a high quality) seems to reduce the number of academically inferior and superior children. I confess that I would want to aim to raise children who are above average in productivity and creativity.

I don't have such specific data from the Soviet Union. The educational and psychological authorities have, in the past, expressed great pride in the day nurseries and boarding institutions for infants and young children. But I think it is significant that they are now emphasizing the contribution of family relationships in the development of sound personalities and admitting that children who are raised in institutions run the risk of "deprivation of psychological stimulation" and of "one-sided or retarded development." The authorities are also discussing the need to go beyond or even reverse the previous primary emphasis in Soviet education on creating the duty-oriented citizen. They stress instead the need to foster the unique potentialities of the individual, so that he may be able to make original or even revolutionary contributions to the society.

In Israel and the Soviet Union the nursery care of babies and young children, so that their mothers can work, is considered patriotic and dignified work. In America such nonprofessional care carries no prestige; as a result, it is very difficult to recruit suitable people here.

So proposals to place babies and children under three years of age in all-day nurseries raise serious questions in the minds of people like myself.

While we are discussing possible new life patterns, we shouldn't assume that the only alternatives for parents are a regular job or being confined to home. Many of the mothers who seek outside work these days are not, I suspect, caught up in the American need to prove themselves with the prestige and pay of a conventional job, yet they do want to engage regularly in some truly meaningful activity in company with other people. It could be painting, choral singing, photography, acting in plays, the study of literature or science, working for justice for a deprived group, building a political movement. The list is endless. Activities such as these enrich the soul as no routine job or passive entertainment can do. Certain of them could be organized by some sort of club or association to which fathers and mothers would go together in the evening—or mothers alone. It could meet in a church basement or in a school. Ideally it would have its own building near a shopping center, large enough to accommodate half a dozen activities simultaneously each night, and a different list every day of the week. There should also be rooms where infants and small children could sleep, and older children could do homework or pursue hobbies. It is just as important that similar activities be available in the daytime for parents caring for their preschool children, in parks, playgrounds, health centers, libraries as well as in churches and shopping centers. Such group activities would be one aspect of the transformation of our neighborhoods into true communities. . . .

I am not thinking here of casual participation in some activity merely for the sake of amusement. I mean a deepening involvement that brings not only increasing skill but a sense of achievement, joy, and growth.

THE FUTURE OF MARRIAGE [8]

Over a century ago, the Swiss historian and ethnologist J. J. Bachofen postulated that early man lived in small packs, ignorant of marriage and indulging in beastlike sexual promiscuity. He could hardly have suggested anything more

[8] From "The Future of Marriage," by Morton Hunt. *Playboy*. 18:116-18+. Ag. '71. Copyright © 1971 by *Playboy*. Originally appeared in *Playboy* magazine. Reprinted by permission. Morton Hunt is the author of several books and has contributed numerous articles to periodicals, many in the field of psychology and changing social patterns.

revolting, or more fascinating, to the puritanical and pru-
rient sensibility of his time, and whole theories of the family
and of society were based on his notion by various anthropologists, as well as by German socialist Friedrich Engels
and Russian revolutionist Pëtr Kropotkin. As the Victorian
fog dissipated, however, it turned out that among the hundreds of primitive peoples still on earth—many of whom
lived much like early man—not a single one was without
some form of marriage and some limitations on the sexual
freedom of the married. Marriage, it appeared, was a genuine
human universal, like speech and social organization.

Nonetheless, Bachofen's myth died hard, because it ap-
pealed to a longing, deep in all of us, for total freedom to
do whatever we want. And recently, it has sprung up from
its own ashes in the form of a startling new notion: Even
if there never was a time when marriage didn't exist, there
soon will be. Lately, the air has been filled with such prophecies of the decline and impending fall of marriage. Some of
the prophets are grieved at this prospect—among them, men
of the cloth, such as the Pope and Dr. Peale, who keep warn-
ing us that hedonism and easy divorce are eroding the very
foundations of family life. Others, who rejoice at the thought,
include an assortment of feminists, hippies and anarchists,
plus much-married theatre people such as Joan Fontaine,
who, having been married more times than the Pope and
Dr. Peale put together, has authoritatively told the world
that marriage is obsolete and that any sensible person can
live and love better without it.

Some of the fire-breathing dragon ladies who have given
Women's Lib an undeservedly bad name urge single women
not to marry and married ones to desert their husbands
forthwith. Kate Millett, the movement's leading theoretician,
expects marriage to wither away after women achieve full
equality. Dr. Roger Egeberg, an Assistant Secretary of HEW
[United States Department of Health, Education, and Wel-
fare], urged Americans in 1969 to reconsider their inherited
belief that everyone ought to marry. And last August [1970],

Mrs. Rita Hauser, the United States representative to the UN Human Rights Commission, said that the idea that marriage was primarily for procreation had become outmoded and that laws banning marriage between homosexuals should be erased from the books.

So much for the voices of prophecy. Are there, in fact, any real indications of a mass revolt against traditional marriage? There certainly seem to be. For one thing, in 1969 there were 660,000 divorces in America—an all-time record— and the divorce rate seems certain to achieve historic new highs in the next few years. For another thing, marital infidelity seems to have increased markedly since Kinsey's first surveys of a generation ago and now is tried, sooner or later, by some 60 percent of married men and 30 to 35 percent of married women in this country. But in what is much more of a departure from the past, infidelity is now tacitly accepted by a fair number of the spouses of the unfaithful. For some couples it has become a shared hobby; mate-swapping and group-sex parties now involve thousands of middle-class marriages. Yet another indication of change is a sharp increase not only in the number of young men and women who, dispensing with legalities, live together unwed but also in the *kind* of people who are doing so; although common-law marriage has long been popular among the poor, in the past few years it has become widespread—and often esteemed —within the middle class.

An even more radical attack on our marriage system is the effort of people in hundreds of communes around the country to construct "families," or group marriages, in which the adults own everything in common, and often consider that they all belong to one another and play mix and match sexually with total freedom. A more complete break with tradition is being made by a rapidly growing percentage of America's male and female homosexuals, who nowadays feel freer than ever to avoid "cover" marriages and to live openly as homosexuals. Their lead is almost certain to be followed by countless others within the next decade or so as our society grows ever more tolerant of personal choice in sexual matters.

Nevertheless, reports of the death of marriage are, to paraphrase Mark Twain, greatly exaggerated. Most human beings regard whatever they grew up with as right and good and see nearly every change in human behavior as a decline in standards and a fall from grace. But change often means adaptation and evolution. The many signs of contemporary revolt against marriage have been viewed as symptoms of a fatal disease, but they may, instead, be signs of a change from an obsolescent form of marriage—patriarchal monogamy—into new forms better suited to present-day human needs.

Marriage as a social structure is exceedingly plastic, being shaped by the interplay of culture and of human needs into hundreds of different forms. In societies where women could do valuable productive work, it often made sense for a man to acquire more than one wife; where women were idle or relatively unproductive—and, hence, a burden—monogamy was more likely to be the pattern. When women had means of their own or could fall back upon relatives, divorce was apt to be easy; where they were wholly dependent on their husbands, it was generally difficult. Under marginal and primitive living conditions, men kept their women in useful subjugation; in wealthier and more leisured societies, women often managed to acquire a degree of independence and power.

For a long while, the only acceptable form of marriage in America was a lifelong one-to-one union, sexually faithful, all but indissoluble, productive of goods and children and strongly husband-dominated. It was a thoroughly functional mechanism during the eighteenth and much of the nineteenth centuries, when men were struggling to secure the land and needed women who would clothe and feed them, produce and rear children to help them, and obey their orders without question for an entire lifetime. It was functional, too, for the women of that time, who, uneducated, unfit for other kinds of work and endowed by law with almost no legal or property rights, needed men who would support them, give them social status and be their guides and protectors for life.

But time passed, the Indians were conquered, the sod was busted, towns and cities grew up, railroads laced the land, factories and offices took the place of the frontier. Less and less did men need women to produce goods and children; more and more, women were educated, had time to spare, made their way into the job market—and realized that they no longer had to cling to their men for life. As patriarchalism lost its usefulness, women began to want and demand orgasms, contraceptives, the vote and respect; men, finding the world growing ever more impersonal and cold, began to want wives who were warm, understanding, companionable and sexy.

Yet, strangely enough, as all these things were happening, marriage not only did not lose ground but grew more popular, and today, when it is under full-scale attack on most fronts, it is more widespread than ever before. A considerably larger percentage of our adult population was married in 1970 than was the case in 1890; the marriage rate, though still below the level of the 1940s, has been climbing steadily since 1963.

The explanation of this paradox is that as marriage was losing its former uses, it was gaining new ones. The changes that were robbing marriage of practical and life-affirming values were turning America into a mechanized urban society in which we felt like numbers, not individuals, in which we had many neighbors but few lifelong friends and in which our lives were controlled by remote governments, huge companies and insensate computers. Alone and impotent, how can we find intimacy and warmth, understanding and loyalty, enduring friendship and a feeling of personal importance? Why, obviously, through *loving* and *marrying*. Marriage is a microcosm, a world within which we seek to correct the shortcomings of the macrocosm around us. St. Paul said it is better to marry than to burn; today, feeling the glacial chill of the world we live in, we find it better to marry than to freeze.

The model of marriage that served the old purposes excellently serves the new ones poorly. But most of the contemporary assaults upon it are not efforts to destroy it; they are efforts to modify and remold it. Only traditional patriarchal marriage is dying, while all around us marriage is being reborn in new forms. The marriage of the future already exists; we have merely mistaken the signs of evolutionary change for the stigmata of necrosis.

Divorce in Perspective

Divorce is a case in point. Far from being a wasting illness, it is a healthful adaptation, enabling monogamy to survive in a time when patriarchal powers, privileges and marital systems have become unworkable; far from being a radical change in the institution of marriage, divorce is a relatively minor modification of it and thoroughly supportive of most of its conventions.

Not that it seemed so at first. When divorce was introduced to Christian Europe, it appeared an extreme and rather sinful measure to most people; even among the wealthy—the only people who could afford it—it remained for centuries quite rare and thoroughly scandalous. In 1816, when president Timothy Dwight of Yale thundered against the "alarming and terrible" divorce rate in Connecticut, about one of every one hundred marriages was being legally dissolved. But as women began achieving a certain degree of emancipation during the nineteenth century, and as the purposes of marriage changed, divorce laws were liberalized and the rate began climbing. Between 1870 and 1905, both the US population and the divorce rate more than doubled; and between then and today, the divorce rate increased over four times.

And not only for the reasons we have already noted but for yet another: the increase in longevity. When people married in their late twenties and marriage was likely to end in death by the time the last child was leaving home, divorce seemed not only wrong but hardly worth the trouble; this was especially true where the only defect in a marriage was boredom. Today, however, when people marry earlier and have finished raising their children with half their adult lives still ahead of them, boredom seems a very good reason for getting divorced.

Half of all divorces occur after eight years of marriage and a quarter of them after fifteen—most of these being not the results of bad initial choices but of disparity or dullness that has grown with time.

Divorcing people, however, are seeking not to escape from marriage for the rest of their lives but to exchange unhappy or boring marriages for satisfying ones. Whatever bitter things they say at the time of divorce, the vast majority do remarry, most of their second marriages lasting the rest of their lives; even those whose second marriages fail are very likely to divorce and remarry again and, that failing, yet again. Divorcing people are actually marrying people, and divorce is not a negation of marriage but a workable cross between traditional monogamy and multiple marriage; sociologists have even referred to it as "serial polygamy."

Despite its costs and its hardships, divorce is thus a compromise between the monogamous ideal and the realities of present-day life. To judge from the statistics, it is becoming more useful and more socially acceptable every year. Although the divorce rate leveled off for a dozen years or so after the postwar surge of 1946, it has been climbing steadily since 1962, continuing the long-range trend of one hundred years, and the rate for the entire nation now stands at nearly one for every three marriages. In some areas, it is even higher. In California, where a new ultraliberal law went into effect in 1970, nearly two of every three marriages end in divorce— a fact that astonishes people in other areas of the country but that Californians themselves accept with equanimity. They still approve of, and very much enjoy, being married;

they have simply gone further than the rest of us in using divorce to keep monogamy workable in today's world.

Seen in the same light, marital infidelity is also a frequently useful modification of the marriage contract rather than a repudiation of it. It violates the conventional moral code to a greater degree than does divorce but, as practiced in America, is only a limited departure from the monogamous pattern. Unfaithful Americans, by and large, neither have extramarital love affairs that last for many years nor do they engage in a continuous series of minor liaisons; rather, their infidelity consists of relatively brief and widely scattered episodes, so that in the course of a married lifetime, they spend many more years being faithful than being unfaithful. Furthermore, American infidelity, unlike its European counterparts, has no recognized status as part of the marital system; except in a few circles, it remains impermissible, hidden and isolated from the rest of one's life.

This is not true at all levels of our society, however: Upper-class men—and, to some extent, women—have long regarded the discreet love affair as an essential complement to marriage, and lower-class husbands have always considered an extracurricular roll in the hay important to a married man's peace of mind. Indeed, very few societies have ever tried to make both husband and wife sexually faithful over a lifetime; the totally monogamous ideal is statistically an abnormality. Professors Clellan Ford and Frank Beach state in *Patterns of Sexual Behavior* that less than 16 percent of 185 societies studied by anthropologists had formal restrictions to a single mate—and, of these, less than a third wholly disapproved of both premarital and extramarital relationships.

Our middle-class, puritanical society, however, has long held that infidelity of any sort is impossible if one truly loves one's mate and is happily married, that any deviation from fidelity stems from an evil or neurotic character and that it inevitably damages both the sinner and the sinned against. This credo drew support from earlier generations of psychotherapists, for almost all the adulterers they treated were neurotic, unhappily married or out of sorts with life in general. But it is just such people who seek psychotherapy; they are hardly a fair sample. Recently, sex researchers have examined the unfaithful more representatively and have come up with quite different findings. Alfred Kinsey, sociologist Robert Whitehurst of Indiana University, sociologist John Cuber of Ohio State University, sexologist/therapist Dr. Albert Ellis and various others (including myself), all of whom have made surveys of unfaithful husbands and wives, agree in general that:

Many of the unfaithful—perhaps even a majority—are not seriously dissatisfied with their marriages nor their mates and a fair number are more or less happily married.

Only about a third—perhaps even fewer—appear to seek extramarital sex for neurotic motives; the rest do so for nonpathological reasons.

Many of the unfaithful—perhaps even a majority—do not feel that they, their mates nor their marriages have been harmed; in my own sample, a tenth said that their marriages had been helped or made more tolerable by their infidelity.

It is still true that many a "deceived" husband or wife, learning about his or her mate's infidelity, feels humiliated, betrayed and unloved, and is filled with rage and the desire for revenge; it is still true, too, that infidelity is a cause in perhaps a third of all divorces. But more often than not, deceived spouses never know of their mates' infidelity nor are their marriages perceptibly harmed by it.

The bulk of present-day infidelity remains hidden beneath the disguise of conventional marital behavior. But an unfettered minority of husbands and wives openly grant each other the right to outside relationships, limiting that right to certain occasions and certain kinds of involvement, in order to keep the marital relationship all-important and unimpaired. A few couples, for instance, take separate vacations or allow each other one night out alone per week, it being understood that their extramarital involvements are to be confined to those times. Similar freedoms have been urged by radical marriage reformers for decades but have never really caught on, and probably never will, for one simple reason: What's out of sight is not necessarily out of mind. What husband can feel sure, despite his wife's promises, that she might not find some other man who will make her dream come true? What wife can feel sure that her husband won't fall in love with some woman he is supposed to be having only a friendly tumble with?

But it's another matter when husband and wife go together in search of extramarital frolic and do their thing with other people, in full view of each other, where it is free of romantic feeling. This is the very essence of marital swinging, or, as it is sometimes called, comarital sex. Whether it consists of a quiet mate exchange between two couples, a small sociable group-sex party or a large orgiastic rumpus, the premise is the same: As long as the extramarital sex is open, shared and purely recreational, it is not considered divisive of marriage. . . .

To the outsider, this must sound very odd, not to say outlandish. How could anyone hope to preserve the warmth and intimacy of marriage by performing the most private and personal sexual acts with other people in front of his own mate or watching his mate do so with others?

Such a question implies that sex is integrally interwoven with the rest of one's feelings about the mate—which it is— but swingers maintain that it can be detached and enjoyed apart from those feelings, without changing them in any way. Marital swinging is supposed to involve only this one segment of the marital relationship and during only a few hours of any week or month; all else is meant to remain intact, monogamous and conventional. . . .

In contrast to this highly specialized and sharply limited attitude, there seems to be a far broader and more thorough rejection of marriage on the part of those men and women who choose to live together unwed. Informal, nonlegal unions have long been widespread among poor blacks, largely for economic reasons, but the present wave of such unions among middle-class whites has an ideological basis, for most of those who choose this arrangement consider themselves revolutionaries who have the guts to pioneer in a more honest and vital relationship than conventional marriage. A forty-four-year-old conference leader, Theodora Wells, and a fifty-one-year-old psychologist, Lee Christie, who live together in Beverly Hills, expounded their philosophy in the April 1970 issue of *The Futurist*:

"Personhood" is central to the living-together relationship; sex roles are central to the marriage relationship. Our experience strongly suggests that personhood excites growth, stimulates openness, increases joyful satisfactions in achieving, encompasses rich, full sexuality peaking in romance. Marriage may have the appearance of this in its romantic phase, but it settles down to prosaic routine. . . . The wife role is diametrically opposed to the personhood I want. I [Theodora] therefore choose to live with the man who joins me in the priority of personhood.

What this means is that she hates homemaking, is career oriented and fears that if she became a legal wife, she would automatically be committed to traditional female roles, to dependency. Hence, she and Christie have rejected marriage and chosen an arrangement without legal obligations, without a head of the household and without a primary money earner or primary homemaker—though Christie, as it happens, does 90 percent of the cooking. Both believe that their freedom from legal ties and their constant need to rechoose each other make for a more exciting, real and growing relationship.

A fair number of the avant-garde and many of the young have begun to find this not only a fashionably rebellious but a thoroughly congenial attitude toward marriage; couples are living together, often openly, on many a college campus, risking punishment by college authorities (but finding the risk smaller every day) and bucking their par-

ents' strenuous disapproval (but getting their glum acceptance more and more often).

When one examines the situation closely, however, it
becomes clear that most of these marital Maoists live together
in close, warm, committed and monogamous fashion, very
much like married people; they keep house together (although often dividing their roles in untraditional ways) and
neither is free to have sex with anyone else, date anyone else
nor even find anyone else intriguing. Anthropologists Margaret Mead and Ashley Montagu, sociologist John Gagnon
and other close observers of the youth scene feel that living
together, whatever its defects, is actually an apprentice marriage and not a true rebellion against marriage at all.

Dr. Mead, incidentally, made a major public pitch in
1966 for a revision of our laws that would create two kinds
of marital status: individual marriage, a legal but easily dissolved form for young people who were unready for parenthood or full commitment to each other but who wanted to
live together with social acceptance; and parental marriage,
a union involving all the legal commitments and responsibilities—and difficulties of dissolution—of marriage as we
presently know it. Her suggestion aroused a great deal of
public debate. The middle-aged, for the most part, condemned her proposal as being an attack upon and a de-
basement of marriage, while the young replied that the
whole idea was unnecessary. The young were right: They
were already creating their own new marital folkway in the
form of the close, serious but informal union that achieved
all the goals of individual marriage except its legality and
acceptance by the middle-aged. Thinking themselves rebels
against marriage, they had only created a new form of marriage closely resembling the very thing Dr. Mead had suggested.

Experiments in Group Marriage

If these modifications of monogamy aren't quite as alarming or as revolutionary as they seem to be, one contemporary

experiment in marriage *is* a genuine and total break with Western tradition. This is group marriage—a catchall term applied to a wide variety of polygamous experiments in which small groups of adult males and females, and their children, live together under one roof or in a close-knit settlement, calling themselves a family, tribe, commune or, more grandly, intentional community and considering themselves all married to one another.

As the term intentional community indicates, these are experiments not merely in marriage but in the building of a new type of society. They are utopian minisocieties existing within, but almost wholly opposed to, the mores and values of present-day American society.

Not that they are all of a piece. A few are located in cities and have members who look and act square and hold regular jobs; some, both urban and rural, consist largely of dropouts, acidheads, panhandlers and petty thieves; but most are rural communities, have hippie-looking members and aim at a self-sufficient farming-and-handicraft way of life. A very few communes are politically conservative, some are in the middle and most are pacifist, anarchistic and/or New Leftist. Nearly all, whatever their national political bent, are islands of primitive communism in which everything is collectively owned and all members work for the common good.

Their communism extends to—or perhaps really begins with—sexual collectivism. Though some communes consist of married couples who are conventionally faithful, many are built around some kind of group sexual sharing. In some of these, couples are paired off but occasionally sleep with other members of the group; in others, pairing off is actively discouraged and the members drift around sexually from one partner to another—a night here, a night there, as they wish.

Group marriage has captured the imagination of many thousands of college students in the past few years through its idealistic and romantic portrayal in three novels widely read by the young—Robert Heinlein's *Stranger in a Strange Land* and Robert Rimmer's *The Harrad Experiment* and *Proposition 31*. The underground press, too, has paid a good deal of sympathetic attention—and the establishment press a good deal of hostile attention—to communes. There has even been, for several years, a West Coast publication titled *The Modern Utopian* that is devoted, in large part, to news and discussions of group marriage. The magazine, which publishes a directory of intentional communities, recently listed 125 communes and the editor said, "For every listing you find here, you can be certain there are 100 others." And an article in the New York *Times* last December [1970] stated that "nearly 2,000 communes in thirty-four states have turned up" but gave this as a conservative figure, as "no accurate count exists."

All this sometimes gives one the feeling that group marriage is sweeping the country; but, based on the undoubtedly exaggerated figures of *The Modern Utopian* and counting a generous average of twenty people per commune, it would still mean that no more than 250,000 adults—approximately one tenth of 1 percent of the US population—are presently involved in group marriages. These figures seem improbable.

Nevertheless, group marriage offers solutions to a number of the nagging problems and discontents of modern monogamy. Collective parenthood—every parent being partly responsible for every child in the group—not only provides a warm and enveloping atmosphere for children but removes some of the pressure from individual parents; moreover, it minimizes the disruptive effects of divorce on the child's world. Sexual sharing is an answer to boredom and solves the problem of infidelity, or seeks to, by declaring extramarital experiences acceptable and admirable. It avoids the success-status-possession syndrome of middle-class family life by turning toward simplicity, communal ownership and communal goals.

Finally, it avoids the loneliness and confinement of monogamy by creating something comparable to what anthropologists call the extended family, a larger grouping of related people living together. (There is a difference, of course: In group marriage, the extended family isn't composed of blood relatives.) Even when sexual switching isn't the focus, there is a warm feeling of being affectionally connected to everyone else. As one young woman in a Taos [New Mexico] commune said ecstatically, "It's really groovy waking up and knowing that forty-eight people love you."

There is, however, a negative side: This drastic reformulation of marriage makes for new problems, some of them more severe than the ones it has solved. Albert Ellis, quoted in Herbert Otto's new book. *The Family in Search of a Future*, lists several categories of serious difficulties with group marriage, including the near impossibility of finding four or more adults who can live harmoniously and lovingly together, the stubborn intrusion of jealousy and love conflicts and the innumerable difficulties of coordinating and scheduling many lives.

Other writers, including those who have sampled communal life, also talk about the problems of leadership (most communes have few rules to start with; those that survive for any time do so by becoming almost conventional and traditional) and the difficulties in communal work sharing (there are always some members who are slovenly and lazy and others who are neat and hard-working, the latter either having to expel the former or give up and let the commune slowly die).

A more serious defect is that most group marriages, being based upon a simple, semiprimitive agrarian life, reintroduce old-style patriarchalism, because such a life puts a premium on masculine muscle power and endurance and leaves the classic domestic and subservient roles to women. Even a most sympathetic observer, psychiatrist Joseph Downing, writes, "In the tribal families, while both sexes work, women are generally in a service role. . . . Male dominance is held desirable by both sexes."

Most serious of all are the emotional limitations of group marriage. Its ideal is sexual freedom and universal love, but the group marriages that most nearly achieve this have the least cohesiveness and the shallowest interpersonal involvements; people come and go, and there is really no marriage at all but only a continuously changing and highly unstable encounter group. The longer-lasting and more cohesive group marriages are, in fact, those in which, as Dr. Downing reports, the initial sexual spree "generally gives way to the quiet, semipermanent, monogamous relationship characteristic of many in our general society."

Not surprisingly, therefore, Dr. Ellis finds that most group marriages are unstable and last only several months to a few years; and sociologist Lewis Yablonsky of California State College at Hayward, who has visited and lived in a number of communes, says that they are often idealistic but rarely successful or enduring. Over and above their specific difficulties, they are utopian—they seek to construct a new society from whole cloth. But all utopias thus far have failed; human behavior is so incredibly complex that every totally new order, no matter how well planned, generates innumerable unforeseen problems. It really is a pity; group living and group marriage look wonderful on paper.

Old-Fashioned Marriage Is Not Dying

All in all, then, the evidence is overwhelming that old-fashioned marriage is not dying and that nearly all of what passes for rebellion against it is a series of patchwork modifications enabling marriage to serve the needs of modern man without being unduly costly or painful.

While this is the present situation, can we extrapolate it into the future? Will marriage continue to exist in some form we can recognize?

It is clear that, in the future, we are going to have an even greater need than we now do for love relationships that offer intimacy, warmth, companionship and a reasonable degree of reliability. Such relationships need not, of course, be heterosexual. With our increasing tolerance of sexual diversity, it seems likely that many homosexual men and women will find it publicly acceptable to live together in quasi-marital alliances.

The great majority of men and women, however, will continue to find heterosexual love the preferred form, for biological and psychological reasons that hardly have to be spelled out here. But need heterosexual love be embodied within marriage? If the world is already badly overpopulated and daily getting worse, why add to its burden—and if one does not intend to have children, why seek to enclose love within a legal cage? Formal promises to love are promises no one can keep, for love is not an act of will; and legal bonds have no power to keep love alive when it is dying.

Such reasoning—more cogent today than ever, due to the climate of sexual permissiveness and to the twin technical advances of the Pill and the loop—lies behind the growth of unwed unions. From all indications, however, such unions will not replace marriage as an institution but only precede it in the life of the individual.

It seems probable that more and more young people will live together unwed for a time and then marry each other or break up and make another similar alliance, and another, until one of them turns into a formal, legal marriage. In fifty years, perhaps less, we may come close to the Scandinavian pattern, in which a great many couples live together prior to marriage. It may be, moreover, that the spread of this practice will decrease the divorce rate among the young, for many of the mistakes that are recognized too late and are undone in divorce court will be recognized and undone outside the legal system, with less social and emotional damage than divorce involves.

If, therefore, marriage continues to be important, what form will it take? The one truly revolutionary innovation is group marriage—and, as we have seen, it poses innumerable and possibly insuperable practical and emotional difficulties. A marriage of one man and one woman involves only one

interrelationship, yet we all know how difficult it is to find
that one right fit and to keep it in working order. But add
one more person, making the smallest possible group marriage, and you have three relationships (A-B, B-C and A-C);
add a fourth to make two couples and you have six relationships; add enough to make a typical group marriage of
fifteen persons and you have 105 relationships.

This is an abstract way of saying that human beings are
all very different and that finding a satisfying and workable
love relationship is not easy, even for a twosome, and is impossibly difficult for aggregations of a dozen or so. It might
prove less difficult, a generation hence, for children brought
up in group marriage communes. Such children would not
have known the close, intense, parent-child relationships of
monogamous marriage and could more easily spread their
affections thinly and undemandingly among many. But this
is mere conjecture, for no communal-marriage experiment
in America has lasted long enough for us to see the results,
except the famous Oneida Community in upstate New York;
it endured from 1848 to 1879, and then its offspring vanished
back into the surrounding ocean of monogamy.

Those group marriages that do endure in the future will
probably be dedicated to a rural and semiprimitive agrarian
life style. Urban communes may last for some years but with
an ever-changing membership and a lack of inner familial
identity; in the city, one's work life lies outside the group,
and with only emotional ties to hold the group together, any
dissension or conflict will result in a turnover of membership. But while agrarian communes may have a sounder
foundation, they can never become a mass movement; there
is simply no way for the land to support well over 200 million people with the low-efficiency productive methods of a
century or two ago.

Agrarian communes not only cannot become a mass
movement in the future but they will not even have much
chance of surviving as islands in a sea of modern industrial-
ism. For semiprimitive agrarianism is so marginal, so back-

breaking and so tedious a way of life that it is unlikely to hold most of its converts against the competing attractions of conventional civilization. Even Dr. Downing, for all his enthusiasm about the "Society of Awakening," as he calls tribal family living, predicts that for the foreseeable future, only a small minority will be attracted to it and that most of these will return to more normal surroundings and relationships after a matter of weeks or months.

Toward a Redefinition of Roles

Thus, monogamy will prevail; on this, nearly all experts agree. But it will almost certainly continue to change in the same general direction in which it has been changing for the past few generations; namely, toward a redefinition of the special roles played by husband and wife, so as to achieve a more equal distribution of the rights, privileges and life expectations of man and woman.

This, however, will represent no sharp break with contemporary marriage, for the marriage of 1971 has come a long way from patriarchy toward the goal of equality. Our prevalent marital style has been termed companionship marriage by a generation of sociologists; in contrast to nineteenth century marriage, it is relatively egalitarian and intimate, husband and wife being intellectually and emotionally close, sexually compatible and nearly equal in personal power and in the quantity and quality of labor each contributes to the marriage.

From an absolute point of view, however, it still is contaminated by patriarchalism. Although each partner votes, most husbands (and wives) still think that men understand politics better; although each may have had similar schooling and believes both sexes to be intellectually equal, most husbands and wives still act as if men were innately better equipped to handle money, drive the car, fill out tax returns and replace fuses. There may be something close to equality in their homemaking, but nearly always it is his career that counts, not hers. If his company wants to move him to another city, she quits her job and looks for another in their new location; and when they want to have children, it is seldom questioned that he will continue to work while she will stay home.

With this, there is a considerable shift back toward traditional role assignments: He stops waxing the floors and washing dishes, begins to speak with greater authority about how their money is to be spent, tells her (rather than consults her) when he would like to work late or take a business trip, gives (or withholds) his approval of her suggestions for parties, vacations and child discipline. The more he takes on the airs of his father, the more she learns to connive and manipulate like her mother. Feeling trapped and discriminated against, resenting the men of the world, she thinks she makes an exception of her husband, but in the hidden recesses of her mind he is one with the others. Bearing the burden of being a man in the world, and resenting the easy life of women, he thinks he makes an exception of his wife but deep down classifies her with the rest.

This is why a great many women yearn for change and what the majority of Women's Liberation members are actively hammering away at. A handful of radicals in the movement think that the answer is the total elimination of marriage, that real freedom for women will come about only through the abolition of legal bonds to men and the establishment of governmentally operated nurseries to rid women once and for all of domestic entrapment. But most women in the movement, and nearly all those outside it, have no sympathy with the antimarriage extremists; they very much want to keep marriage alive but aim to push toward completion the evolutionary trends that have been under way so long.

Concretely, women want their husbands to treat them as equals; they want help and participation in domestic duties; they want help with child rearing; they want day-care centers and other agencies to free them to work at least part time, while their children are small, so that they won't have to give up their careers and slide into the imprisonment of domesticity. They want an equal voice in all the decisions made in the home—including job decisions that affect married life; they want their husbands to respect them, not indulge them; they want, in short, to be treated as if they were their husbands' best friends—which, in fact, they are, or should be.

Does the "New Marriage" Demand Too Much

All this is only a continuation of the developments in marriage over the past century and a quarter. The key question is: How far can marriage evolve in this direction without making excessive demands upon both partners? Can most husbands and wives have full-time uninterrupted careers, share all the chores and obligations of homemaking and parenthood and still find time for the essential business of love and companionship?

From the time of the early suffragettes, there have been women with the drive and talent to be full-time doctors, lawyers, retailers and the like, and at the same time to run a home and raise children with the help of housekeepers, nannies and selfless husbands. From these examples, we can judge how likely this is to become the dominant pattern of the future. Simply put, it isn't, for it would take more energy, money and good luck than the great majority of women possess and more skilled helpers than the country could possibly provide. But what if child care were more efficiently handled in state-run centers, which would make the totally egalitarian marriage much more feasible? The question then becomes: How many middle-class American women would really prefer full-time work to something less demanding that would give them more time with their children? The truth is that most of the world's work is dull and wearisome rather than exhilarating and inspiring. Women's Lib leaders are largely middle-to-upper-echelon professionals, and no wonder they think every wife would be better off working full time—but we have yet to hear the same thing from saleswomen, secretaries and bookkeepers.

Married women *are* working more all the time—in 1970, over half of all mothers whose children were in school held jobs—but the middle-class women among them pick and choose things they like to do rather than *have* to do for a living; moreover, many work part time until their children have grown old enough to make mothering a minor assignment. Accordingly, they make much less money than their husbands, rarely ever rise to any high positions in their fields and, to some extent, play certain traditionally female roles within marriage. It is a compromise and, like all compromises, it delights no one—but serves nearly everyone better than more clear-cut and idealistic solutions.

Though the growth of egalitarianism will not solve all the problems of marriage, it may help solve the problems of a *bad* marriage. With their increasing independence, fewer and fewer wives will feel compelled to remain confined within unhappy or unrewarding marriages. Divorce, therefore, can be expected to continue to increase, despite the offsetting effect of extramarital liaisons. Extrapolating the rising divorce rate, we can conservatively expect that within another generation, half or more of all persons who marry will be divorced at least once. But even if divorce were to become an almost universal experience, it would not be the *antithesis* of marriage but only a part of the marital experience; most people will, as always, spend their adult lives married —not continuously, in a single marriage, but segmentally, in two or more marriages. For all the dislocations and pain these divorces cause, the sum total of emotional satisfaction in the lives of the divorced and remarried may well be greater than their great-grandparents were able to achieve.

Marital infidelity, since it also relieves some of the pressures and discontents of unsuccessful or boring marriages— and does so in most cases without breaking up the existing home—will remain an alternative to divorce and will probably continue to increase, all the more so as women come to share more fully the traditional male privileges. Within another generation, based on present trends, four of five husbands and two of three wives whose marriages last more than several years will have at least a few extramarital involvements.

Overt permissiveness, particularly in the form of marital swinging, may be tried more often than it now is, but most of those who test it out will do so only briefly rather than adopt it as a way of life. Swinging has a number of built-in difficulties, the first and most important of which is that the avoidance of all emotional involvement—the very keystone of swinging—is exceedingly hard to achieve. Nearly all professional observers report that jealousy is a frequent and severely disruptive problem. . . .

There will be wider and freer variations in marital styles —we are a pluralistic nation, growing more tolerant of diversity all the time—but throughout all the styles of marriage in the future will run a predominant motif that has been implicit in the evolution of marriage for a century and a quarter and that will finally come to full flowering in a generation or so. In short, the marriage of the future will be a heterosexual friendship, a free and unconstrained union of a man and a woman who are companions, partners, comrades and sexual lovers. There will still be a certain degree of specialization within marriage, but by and large, the daily business of living together—the talk, the meals, the going out to work and coming home again, the spending of money, the lovemaking, the caring for the children, even the indulgence or nonindulgence in outside affairs—will be governed by this fundamental relationship rather than by the lord-and-servant relationship of patriarchal marriage. Like all friendships, it will exist only as long as it is valid; it will rarely last a lifetime, yet each marriage, while it does last, will meet the needs of the men and women of the future as no earlier form of marriage could have. Yet we who know the marriage of today will find it relatively familiar, comprehensible—and very much alive.

WHAT IT WOULD BE LIKE IF WOMEN WIN [9]

Any change is fearful, especially one affecting both politics and sex roles, so let me begin these utopian speculations with a fact. To break the ice.

Women don't want to exchange places with men. Male chauvinists, science-fiction writers and comedians may favor that idea for its shock value, but psychologists say it is a fantasy based on ruling-class ego and guilt. Men assume that women want to imitate them, which is just what white people assumed about blacks. An assumption so strong that it may convince the second-class group of the need to imitate, but for both women and blacks that stage has passed. Guilt produces the question: What if they could treat us as we have treated them?

That is not our goal. But we do want to change the economic system to one more based on merit. [In Women's Lib Utopia, there will be free access to good jobs—and decent pay for the bad ones women have been performing all along, including housework. Increased skilled labor might lead to a four-hour workday, and higher wages would encourage further mechanization of repetitive jobs now kept alive by cheap labor.

With women as half the country's elected representatives, and a woman President once in a while, the country's *machismo* problems would be greatly reduced. The old-fashioned idea that manhood depends on violence and victory is, after all, an important part of our troubles in the streets, and in Vietnam. I'm not saying that women leaders would eliminate violence. We are not more moral than men; we are only uncorrupted by power so far. When we do acquire power, we might turn out to have an equal impulse toward aggression. Even now, Margaret Mead believes that women fight less often but more fiercely than men, because women

[9] Article by Gloria Steinem, a contributing editor of *New York Magazine* and feminist leader. *Time*. 96:22-3. Ag. 31, '70. Reprinted by permission from *Time*, The Weekly Newsmagazine; Copyright Time Inc., 1970.

are not taught the rules of the war game and fight only
when cornered. But for the next fifty years or so, women in
politics will be very valuable by tempering the idea of manhood into something less aggressive and better suited to this
crowded, postatomic planet. Consumer protection and children's rights, for instance, might get more legislative attention.

Men will have to give up ruling-class privileges, but in
return they will no longer be the only ones to support the
family, get drafted, bear the strain of power and responsibility. Freud to the contrary, anatomy is not destiny, at least
not for more than nine months at a time. In Israel, women
are drafted, and some have gone to war. In England, more
men type and run switchboards. In India and Israel, a
woman rules. In Sweden, both parents take care of the children. In this country, come Utopia, men and women won't
reverse roles; they will be free to choose according to individual talents and preferences.

If role reform sounds sexually unsettling, think how it
will change the sexual hypocrisy we have now. No more sex
arranged on the barter system, with women pretending interest, and men never sure whether they are loved for themselves or for the security few women can get any other way.
(Married or not, for sexual reasons or social ones, most
women still find it second nature to Uncle Tom.) No more
men who are encouraged to spend a lifetime living with
inferiors; with housekeepers, or dependent creatures who are
still children. No more domineering wives, emasculating
women, and "Jewish mothers," all of whom are simply human beings with all their normal ambition and drive confined to the home. No more unequal partnerships that
eventually doom love and sex.

In order to produce that kind of confidence and individ-
uality, child rearing will train according to talent. Little
girls will no longer be surrounded by airtight, self-fulfilling
prophecies of natural passivity, lack of ambition and objec-
tivity, inability to exercise power, and dexterity (so long as

special aptitude for jobs requiring patience and dexterity is confined to poorly paid jobs; brain surgery is for males).

Schools and universities will help to break down traditional sex roles, even when parents will not. Half the teachers will be men, a rarity now at preschool and elementary levels; girls will not necessarily serve cookies or boys hoist up the flag. Athletic teams will be picked only by strength and skill. Sexually segregated courses like auto mechanics and home economics will be taken by boys and girls together. New courses in sexual politics will explore female subjugation as the model for political oppression, and women's history will be an academic staple, along with black history, at least until the white-male-oriented textbooks are integrated and rewritten.

As for the American child's classic problem—too much mother, too little father—that would be cured by an equalization of parental responsibility. Free nurseries, school lunches, family cafeterias built into every housing complex, service companies that will do household cleaning chores in a regular, businesslike way, and more responsibility by the entire community for the children: all these will make it possible for both mother and father to work, and to have equal leisure time with the children at home. For parents of very young children, however, a special job category, created by government and unions, would allow such parents a shorter work day.

The revolution would not take away the option of being a housewife. A woman who prefers to be her husband's housekeeper and/or hostess would receive a percentage of his pay determined by the domestic relations courts. If divorced, she might be eligible for a pension fund, and for a job-training allowance. Or a divorce could be treated the same way that the dissolution of a business partnership is now.

If these proposals seem farfetched, consider Sweden, where most of them are already in effect. Sweden is not yet a working Women's Lib model; most of the role-reform

programs began less than a decade ago, and are just beginning to take hold. But that country is so far ahead of us in
recognizing the problem that Swedish statements on sex and
equality sound like bulletins from the moon.

Our marriage laws, for instance, are so reactionary that
Women's Lib groups want couples to take a compulsory
written exam on the law, as for a driver's license, before
going through with the wedding. A man has alimony and
wifely debts to worry about, but a woman may lose so many
of her civil rights that in the United States now, in important
legal ways, she becomes a child again. In some states, she
cannot sign credit agreements, use her maiden name, incor-
porate a business, or establish a legal residence of her own.
Being a wife, according to most social and legal definitions,
is still a nineteenth century thing.

Assuming, however, that these blatantly sexist laws are
abolished or reformed, that job discrimination is forbidden,
that parents share financial responsibility for each other and
the children, and that sexual relationships become partnerships of equal adults (some pretty big assumptions), then
marriage will probably go right on. Men and women are,
after all, physically complementary. When society stops en-
couraging men to be exploiters and women to be parasites,
they may turn out to be more complementary in emotion as
well. Women's Lib is not trying to destroy the American
family. A look at the statistics on divorce—plus the way in
which old people are farmed out with strangers and young
people flee the home—shows the destruction that has already
been done. Liberated women are just trying to point out the
disaster, and build compassionate and practical alternatives
from the ruins.

What will exist is a variety of alternative life-styles. Since
the population explosion dictates that childbearing be kept
to a minimum, parents-and-children will be only one of
many "families": couples, age groups, working groups, mixed
communes, blood-related clans, class groups, creative groups.
Single women will have the right to stay single without ridi-

cule, without the attitudes now betrayed by "spinster" and "bachelor." Lesbians or homosexuals will no longer be denied legally binding marriages, complete with mutual-support agreements and inheritance rights. Paradoxically, the number of homosexuals may get smaller. With fewer overpossessive mothers and fewer fathers who hold up an impossibly cruel or perfectionist idea of manhood, boys will be less likely to be denied or reject their identity as males.

Changes that now seem small may get bigger:

Men's Lib. Men now suffer from more diseases due to stress, heart attacks, ulcers, a higher suicide rate, greater difficulty living alone, less adaptability to change and, in general, a shorter life span than women. There is some scientific evidence that what produces physical problems is not work itself, but the inability to choose which work, and how much. With women bearing half the financial responsibility, and with the idea of "masculine" jobs gone, men might well feel freer and live longer.

Religion. Protestant women are already becoming ordained ministers; radical nuns are carrying out liturgical functions that were once the exclusive property of priests; Jewish women are rewriting prayers—particularly those that Orthodox Jews recite every morning thanking God they are not female. In the future, the church will become an area of equal participation by women. This means, of course, that organized religion will have to give up one of its great historical weapons: sexual repression. In most structured faiths, from Hinduism through Roman Catholicism, the status of women went down as the position of priests ascended. Male clergy implied, if they did not teach, that women were unclean, unworthy and sources of ungodly temptation, in order to remove them as rivals for the emotional forces of men. Full participation of women in ecclesiastical life might involve certain changes in theology, such as, for instance, a radical redefinition of sin.

Literary problems. Revised sex roles will outdate more children's books than civil rights ever did. Only a few children had the problem of a *Little Black Sambo*, but most have the male-female stereotypes of "Dick and Jane." A boomlet of children's books about mothers who work has already begun, and liberated parents and editors are beginning to pressure for change in the textbook industry. Fiction writing will change more gradually, but romantic novels with wilting heroines and swashbuckling heroes will be reduced to historical value. Or perhaps to the sado-masochist trade. (*Marjorie Morningstar,* a romantic novel that took the fifties by storm, has already begun to seem as unreal as its twenties predecessor, *The Sheik.*) As for the literary plots that turn on forced marriages or horrific abortions, they will seem as dated as Prohibition stories. Free legal abortions and free birth control will force writers to give up pregnancy as the *deus ex machina.*

Manners and Fashion. Dress will be more androgynous, with class symbols becoming more important than sexual ones. Pro- or anti-Establishment styles may already be more vital than who is wearing them. Hardhats are just as likely to rough up antiwar girls as antiwar men in the street, and police understand that women are just as likely to be pushers or bombers. Dances haven't required that one partner lead the other for years, anyway. Chivalry will transfer itself to those who need it, or deserve respect: old people, admired people, anyone with an armload of packages. Women with normal work identities will be less likely to attach their whole sense of self to youth and appearance; thus there will be fewer nervous breakdowns when the first wrinkles appear. Lighting cigarettes and other treasured niceties will become gestures of mutual affection. "I like to be helped on with my coat," says one Women's Lib worker, "but not if it costs me $2,000 a year in salary."

For those with nostalgia for a simpler past, here is a word of comfort. Anthropologist Geoffrey Gorer studied the few peaceful human tribes and discovered one common characteristic: sex roles were not polarized. Differences of dress and occupation were at a minimum. Society, in other words, was not using sexual blackmail as a way of getting women to do cheap labor, or men to be aggressive.

Thus Women's Lib may achieve a more peaceful society on the way toward its other goals. That is why the Swedish government considers reform to bring about greater equality in the sex roles one of its most important concerns. As Prime Minister Olof Palme explained in a widely ignored speech delivered in Washington this spring: "It is *human beings* we shall emancipate. In Sweden today, if a politician should declare that the woman ought to have a different role from man's, he would be regarded as something from the Stone Age." In other words, the most radical goal of the movement is egalitarianism.

If Women's Lib wins, perhaps we all do.

BIBLIOGRAPHY

An asterisk (*) preceding a reference indicates that the article or a part of it has been reprinted in this book.

BOOKS, PAMPHLETS, AND DOCUMENTS

Adorno, T. W. and others. The authoritarian personality. Harper. '50.

Asch, S. E. Studies of independence and conformity, pt 1: A minority of one against a unanimous majority. (Psychological Monographs: general and applied, v 70, no 9) American Psychological Association. '56.

Baker, E. F. Technology and woman's work. Columbia University Press. '64.

Bardwick, J. M. and others. Feminine personality and conflict. Brooks/Cole. '70.

Beauvoir, Simone de. The second sex; tr. and ed. by H. M. Parshley. Modern Lib. '68.
    Copyright 1952

Benson, M. S. Women in eighteenth century America. Kennikat. '66.

Beshiri, P. H. The woman doctor. Cowles. '69.

Bettelheim, Bruno. Symbolic wounds; puberty rites and the envious male. new, rev. ed. Collier. '62.

Bird, Caroline. Born female; the high cost of keeping women down. McKay. '68.

Blood, R. O. and Wolfe, D. M. Husbands and wives. Free Press. '60.

Cade, Toni, comp. The Black woman; an anthology. New American Lib. '70.

Cain, G. G. Married women in the labor force. University of Chicago Press. '66.

Cisler, Lucinda. Women: a bibliography. 5th ed. rev. and enl. The author. 102 W. 80th St. New York 10024. '69.

Cross, B. M. ed. The educated woman in America. Teachers College Press. '65.

Deutsch, Helene. The psychology of women: a psychoanalytical interpretation. Grune and Stratton. '44.

Duverger, Maurice. The political role of women. UNESCO. '55.

Farber, S. M. and Wilson, R. H. L. eds. The challenge to women. Basic Books. '66.

Farber, S. M. and Wilson, R. H. L. eds. The potential of women; symposium. (Man and Civilization symposia) McGraw. '63.
   Woman's intellect. E. E. Maccoby. p 24-39.

Flexner, Eleanor. A century of struggle: the woman's rights movement in the United States. Harvard University Press. '59; paper ed. Atheneum. '68.

Friedan, Betty. The feminine mystique. Dell. '65.

*Garskof, M. H. ed. Roles women play: readings toward women's liberation. Brooks/Cole. '71.
   Reprinted in this book: The social construction of the second sex. Jo Freeman. p 123-41.
   See also Femininity and successful achievement: a basic inconsistency. M. S. Horner. p 97-122; Equality between the sexes: an immodest proposal. A. S. Rossi. p 145-64.

Ginzberg, Eli and others. Life styles of educated women. Columbia University Press. '66.

Goode, W. J. The family. Prentice-Hall. '64.

Greer, Germaine. The female eunuch. McGraw. '71.
   Review. National Observer. p 6. Jl. 9, '71. Wesley Pruden.

Harbeson, G. E. Choice and challenge for the American woman. Schenkman. '67.

Horney, Karen. Feminine psychology. Norton. '67.

Humphrey, Grace. Women in American history. Books for Libs. '68.
   Copyright 1919

International Encyclopedia of the Social Sciences. Macmillan. '68.
   V 7, p 207-13. Individual differences—Sex differences. L. Tyler.

Janeway, Elizabeth. Man's world, woman's place: a study in social mythology. Morrow. '71.

Kagan, Jerome, and Moss, H. A. Birth to maturity. Wiley. '62.

Kanowitz, Leo. Women and the law. University of New Mexico Press. '69.

Kraditor, A. S. ed. Up from the pedestal. Quadrangle. '68.

Lamson, Peggy. Few are chosen. Houghton. '68.

Leonard, E. A. A. The dear-bought heritage. University of Pennsylvania Press. '65.

Lifton, R. J. ed. The woman in America. Houghton. '65.

McClelland, D. C. The achieving society. Van Nostrand. '61.

Maccoby, E. E. ed. The development of sex differences. Stanford University Press. '66.

Mailer, Norman. The prisoner of sex. Little. '71.
   Originally published in Harper's Magazine. 242:41-6+. Mr. '71.

Mattfeld, J. A. and Van Aken, C. G. eds. Women and the scientific professions. Massachusetts Institute of Technology. '65.

Merriam, Eve ed. Growing up female in America: ten lives. Doubleday. '71.

Millett, Kate. Sexual politics. Doubleday. '70.

Montagu, Ashley. The natural superiority of women. rev. ed. Macmillan. '68.

Myrdal, A. R. and Klein, Viola. Women's two roles. 2d ed. rev. Humanities Press. '68.

Myrdal, Gunnar. An American dilemma: the Negro problem and modern democracy. 20th anniversary ed. Harper. '62.
    Appendix 5. p 1073-8. A parallel to the Negro problem.

Nye, F. I. and Hoffman, L. N. W. eds. The employed mother in America. Rand McNally. '63.
    Employment and the adolescent. Elizabeth Douvan. p 142-64.

Odenwald, R. P. The disappearing sexes. Random House. '66.

O'Neill, B. P. Careers for women after marriage and children. Macmillan. '65.

O'Neill, W. L. Everyone was brave; the rise and fall of feminism in America. Quadrangle. '69.
    Essay review. Saturday Review. 52:27-9+. O. 11, '69. Elizabeth Janeway.

O'Neill, W. L. The woman movement. Barnes & Noble. '69.

Pierce, J. V. Sex differences in achievement motivation of able high school students. (Cooperative Research Project. No. 1097) Chicago. '61.

Porter, K. H. A history of suffrage in the United States. Greenwood Press. '69.

Proshansky, H. M. and Seidenberg, Bernard, eds. Basic studies in social psychology. Holt. '65.
    The relation of need for achievement to learning experiences in independence and mastery. M. R. Winterbottom. p 294-308.

Riegel, R. E. American feminists. University of Kansas Press. '69.

Scofield, N. E. and Klarman, Betty. So you want to go back to work! Random House. '68.

*Spock, Benjamin. Decent and indecent; our personal and political behavior. rev. ed. Fawcett. '71.
    Originally published in 1970 by McCall Publishing Company.

United States. President's Commission on the Status of Women. American women; ed. by Margaret Mead and F. B. Kaplan. Scribner. '65.

*United States. Women's Bureau. Trends in educational attainment of women. The Bureau. Washington, D.C. 20210. '69.

Woman's Rights Convention, Seneca Falls, N.Y., 1848. Woman's rights conventions, Seneca Falls & Rochester, 1848. Arno. '69.
    Reprint of the 1870 ed.
Woody, Thomas. A history of women's education in the United States. Octagon Books. '66. 2v.

Periodicals

America. 123:144-6. S. 12, '70. How to unnerve male chauvinists. Edward Glynn.

American Education. 6:3-6. D. '70. Move over, gents. E. J. Simpson.

American Journal of Economics. 28:271-84. Jl. '69. Monetary value of a housewife: an economic analysis for use in litigation. C. S. Pyun.

American Journal of Sociology. 74:392-407. Ja. '69. Working wives and marriage happiness. S. R. Orden and N. M. Bradburn.
    Reply with rejoinder. American Journal of Sociology. 75:412-15. N. '69. M. Poloma and T. Garland.

American Journal of Sociology. 75:965-82. My. '70. Encountering the male establishment; sex-status limits on women's careers in the professions. C. F. Epstein.

American Scholar. 33:355-75. Summer '64. An American anachronism: the image of women and work. Ellen Keniston and Kenneth Keniston.

American Scholar. 40:235-48. Spring '71. Women's rights and American feminism. Gerda Lerner.

American Sociological Review. 33:750-60. O. '68. Do American women marry up? Zick Rubin.
    Discussion. American Sociological Review. 34:725-8. O. '69; 35:327-8. Ap. '70

Business Week. p 42-4+. Ag. 2, '69. For women, a difficult climb to the top.

Business Week. p 18-19. S. 5, '70. How bosses feel about women's lib: job policies unaffected.

Christian Science Monitor. p 1+. Ap. 24, '70. Women's liberation: where to next. Marilyn Hoffman; Patricia Shelton.

Christian Science Monitor. p 9. Ag. 22-24, '70. What will women do with the '70s.

*Christian Science Monitor. p 10. Mr. 22, '71. Still inequalities in socialist society.

Christian Science Monitor. p 4. Jl. 23, '71. Black woman breaks barriers in library. Aline Wilbur.

Christian Science Monitor. p 4. Jl. 23, '71. Marital guidance for Swedes. Pamela Marsh.

Christian Science Monitor. p 4. Jl. 23, '71. Trade union leader. Niti Salloway.

Christian Science Monitor. p 10. O. 12, '71. These scholars surprise Peking. Cheryl Payer.

Christian Science Monitor. p 12. O. 19, '71. Why not pensions for housewives, too? H. B. Ellis.

Christian Science Monitor. p 14. O. 29, '71. Swiss women due for first federal vote. Margaret Patterson.

Christian Science Monitor. p 8. N. 2, '71. Norwegian women wield ballots. I. N. Means.

Christian Science Monitor. p 14. N. 9, '71. UN's unique assembly ... of wordly wise women.

Christian Science Monitor. p 6. N. 23, '71. Woman studies gain toehold on campuses.

Christian Science Monitor. p 6. N. 23, '71. Women's legal status explored. L. J. Leith.

Commentary. 50:33-44. O. '70. The liberated woman. Midge Decter.

Commentary. 51:63-8. Mr. '71. Sexism in the head. Arlene Croce.

*Conference Board Record (National Industrial Conference Board). 7:37-9. Ap. '70. Women in the labor force. Fabian Linden.

Congressional Digest. 50:1-32. Ja. '71. This month's feature: Congress and the equal rights amendment.

*Editorial Research Reports. 2, no 4:545-62. Jl. 24, '70. Abortion law reform. R. L. Worsnop.

*Editorial Research Reports. 2, no 5:565-85. Ag. 5, '70. Status of women. H. B. Shaffer.

Esquire. 75:82-5+. Ja. '71. Feminine mistake. Helen Lawrenson.
    Reply. Esquire. 75:22. Mr. '71. Caroline Bird.

*Fortune. 83:76-9. F. '71. There are sex differences of the mind, too. Tom Alexander.

Good Housekeeping. 171:73-5. N. '70. It's still a man's world, with reports by seven women who speak out. L. C. Pogrebin.

Historian. 32:210-27. F. '70. Subtle subversion: changes in the traditionalist image of the American woman. G. G. Riley.

Human Relations. 22:3-30. F. '69. Dual career family: a variant pattern and social change. Rhona Rapoport and R. N. Rapoport.

Journal of Abnormal and Social Psychology. 55:327-32. N. '57. A cross-cultural survey of some sex differences in socialization. Herbert Barry III, M. K. Bacon, and I. L. Child.

Journal of Genetic Psychology. 54:17-25. Mr. '39. Age and sex differences in children's opinion concerning sex differences. Stevenson Smith.

Journal of Marriage and the Family. 27:43-7. F. '65. Long-range causes and consequences of the employment of married women. R. O. Blood.

Journal of Marriage and the Family. 28:200-3. My. '66. An analysis of power dynamics in marriage. P. N. Hallenbeck.

Journal of Marriage and the Family. 31:65-72. F. '69. Working-class wives in suburbia: fulfillment or crisis? Irving Tallman.

Journal of Marriage and the Family. 32:242-9. My. '70. Career salience and atypicality of occupational choice among college women. E. M. Almquist and S. S. Angrist.

Journal of Marriage and the Family. 32:457-64. Ag. '70. Working wife: differences in perception among Negro and white males. L. J. Axelson.

Ladies Home Journal. 87:63-71. Ag. '70. New feminism [with editorial comment].

Library Journal. 96:2587-94. S. 1, '71. Sisterhood is serious: an annotated bibliography. Pat Schuman and Gay Detlefsen.

Library Journal. 96:2597-9. S. 1, '71. A healthy anger. Helen Lowenthal.

Library Journal. 96:2600-3. S. 1, '71. The legal status of women. K. A. Cassell.

Life. 70:30-3. My. 7, '71. Germaine Greer. Jordan Bonfante.

*Life. 71:48-55. Ag. 13, '71. Where did it all go wrong? Richard Gilman.

Look. 34:15-17. S. 22, '70. Motherhood, who needs it? Betty Rollin.

Look. 35:73+. Ja. 26, '71. Executive mother: Joan Glynn. Louis Botto.

*Look. 35:15-19. Mr. 9, '71. Backlash against Women's Lib! "They're a bunch of frustrated hags." Betty Rollin.

Look. 35:11. Ap. 6, '71. Men, women, and politics. Lenore Romney.

*Los Angeles Times. p E 1. N. 29, '70. Man's primer to Womlib. Maggie Savoy.

*Los Angeles Times. p 1. Ap. 18, '71. The working mother's crises. M. L. Loper.

McCall's. 96:69+. My. '69. Are we the last married generation? Harriet Van Horne.

McCall's. 97:128. S. '70. Report on the status of women. Susanna McBee.

McCall's. 98:85-7. F. '71. Where the women are. Shana Alexander.

McCall's. 98:90-5. F. '71. Women's legal rights in 50 states.

Mental Hygiene. 55:1-9. Ja. '71. Mental health movement meets Women's Lib; special symposium. Ethel Tobach; Natalie Shainess; Dorothy Headley.

Metropolitan Life Statistical Bulletin. 51:5-7. Ja. '70. Profile of the American wife.

Monthly Labor Review. 92:31-5. O. '69. Married women in the labor force: an analysis of participation rates. M. S. Cohen.

Ms. Preview issue [D. 20, '71].
    Bound in New York Magazine. 4:43-86. D. 20, '71.

National Observer. p 1+. Mr. 9, '71. The compleat revolution: restructure everything, the new feminists demand. Jim Hampton.

Nation's Business. 58:80-8. N. '70. Those powerful powder puff executives; nine top women executives. S. G. Slappey.

New Republic. 163:15-17. O. 10, '70. Help. Janet Malcolm.
    Discussion. New Republic. 163:40-5. O. 31, '70.

New Statesman. 80:561. O. 30, '70. They want it now. Mervyn Jones.

New York Magazine. 4:26-30. F. 22, '71. The march of *Time*'s women. Lilla Lyon.

New York Magazine. 4:10-11. Mr. 1, '71. Divorced mothers as a political force. Gail Sheehy.

New York Magazine. 4:44-9. Mr. 1, '71. Divorce by the books. Jane O'Reilly.

New York Magazine. 4:43-7. Mr. 15, '71. Television's femininity gap. Winnie Stark.

*New York Times. p 24. N. 8, '67. U.N. Declaration on Women's Rights [text].

New York Times. p 30. F. 4, '70. The women who'd trade in their pedestal for total equality. Marylin Bender.

New York Times. p 33. Jl. 31, '70. Doctors deny woman's hormones affect her as an executive. Marylin Bender.

New York Times. p 29. Ag. 21, '70. Liberation yesterday—the roots of the feminist movement. Marylin Bender.

New York Times. p 33. D. 22, '70. The media and male chauvinism. Robin Morgan.

*New York Times. p 1. Ja. 31, '71. Job bias against women easing under pressure. J. M. Flint.

New York Times. p 35. Mr. 22, '71. Moscow is split on nursery issue.

New York Times. p 55. Mr. 28, '71. Day care is urged to ease mothers' "drudgery." J. F. Clarity.

New York Times. p 28. Ap. 7, '71. A look at women's lib in suburbia: the emphasis is different.

*New York Times. p 1. Ap. 11, '71. For women, a decade of widening horizons. Jack Rosenthal.

New York Times. p F 2. My. 2, '71. Maternity leave: an employe right? Marylin Bender.

New York Times. p 44. My. 27, '71. Why is it "man's world and woman's place?" V. L. Warren.

New York Times. p 47. Je. 14, '71. Women executives who mind the store. Bernadine Morris.

New York Times. p 41. Je. 17, '71. The human lib movement: I. Warren Farrell.

*New York Times. p 1. Jl. 13, '71. Women's job rights gain in Federal court rulings. Eileen Shanahan.

New York Times. p 32. Ag. 11, '71. The future of the American family: despite all, Dr Brothers sees hope. R. M. Thomas, Jr.

New York Times. p 60. S. 30, '71. Out to debunk "the motherhood myth." J. E. Brody.

New York Times. p 43+. O. 1, '71. A women's lib parable—of 449 B.C. Henry Raymont.

New York Times. p 39. O. 4, '71. Ethel Strainchamps wrote this [discussion of nomenclature].

New York Times. p 1+. O. 13, '71. Equal rights amendment passed by House, 354-23.

New York Times. p 1+. O. 22, '71. President bypasses women for the Court; talent pool small. Eileen Shanahan.

New York Times. p 35. O. 22, '71. MS isn't sweeping the nation, the foes of Miss/Mrs. find. Enid Nemy.

New York Times. p D 17. O. 31, '71. "I want to work with women." Jane Fonda.

New York Times. p 1+. N. 23, '71. [Supreme] Court, for first time, overrules a state law that favors men. F. P. Graham.

New York Times Magazine. p 35-7+. O. 25, '70. Male dominance? Yes, alas. A sexist plot? No. Lionel Tiger.
    Discussion. New York Times Magazine. p 26+ N. 15; 22+ N. 22 '70.

New York Times Magazine. p 27-9+. N. 29, '70. Mother superior to Women's lib: Betty Friedan. Paul Wilkes.
    Reply with rejoinder. New York Times Magazine. p 44+. Ja. 24, '71. Lucy Komisar.

New York Times Magazine. p 4-5+. Jl. 11, '71. Europe's first feminist has changed the second sex. Curtis Cate.

New Yorker. 46:52-6+. N. 28, '70. Profiles; founding cadre: personalities of and dialogues among some members of a women's liberation group. Jane Kramer.

*Newsweek. 76:81. N. 2, '70. Faith of our feminists; question of ordination.

Newsweek. 77:70. Ja. 11, '71. Women's gains; annual survey of employment.

*Playboy. 18:116-18+. Ag. '71. The future of marriage. Morton Hunt.

Psychiatry. 9:69-71. F. '46. Anti-feminism and race prejudice. Ashley Montagu.

Psychology Today. 3:36-8+. N. '69. Fail: bright women. M. S. Horner.

Psychology Today. 4:22+ N. '70. We're all nonconscious sexists. S. L. Bem and D. J. Bem.

PTA Magazine. 65:6-8. Ja. '71. How men will benefit from the women's power revolution. Marya Mannes.

Publishers Weekly. 199:20-2. Mr. 22, '71. Only you, Dick Daring! Survival report on NBA Week: sexism (sic) in children's books [report of panel discussion].

*Saturday Review. 52:29. O. 11, '69. What did the Nineteenth Amendment amend? Rochelle Girson.

Saturday Review. 53:22-3+. Ag. 29, '70. Fettered and stunted by patriarchy. Muriel Haynes.

*Saturday Review. 53:16-18+. O. 10, '70. Female biology in a male culture. Diana Trilling.

Saturday Review. 54:16-19. Ja. 9, '71. The sexes: getting it all together. Faubion Bowers.

Saturday Review. 54:47-9+. F. 20, '71. A timid giant grows bolder. B. M. Caldwell.

Saturday Review. 54:76-7+. O. 16, '71. Sexual stereotypes start early. Florence Howe.

Saturday Review. 54:83-6+. O. 16, '71. Woman's place is in the curriculum. J. L. Trecker.

Science. 170:413-16. O. 23, '70. Psychological and social barriers to women in science; adaptation of address. November 22, 1969. M. S. White.

Science. 170:834-5. N. 20, '70. Sex discrimination: campuses face contract loss over HEW demands. R. J. Bazell.
    Reply. Science. 171:236. Ja. 22, '71. Florence Moog.

Senior Scholastic. 97:7-12. N. 9, '70. American woman: history and HERstory.

Senior Scholastic. 97:13-14. N. 9, '70. Who's she? women activists in U.S. history.

Social Forces. 30:60-9. O. '51. Women as a minority group. H. M. Hacker.

Time. 96:43-4. Ag. 3, '70. Strengthening the weaker sex.

*Time. 96:22-3. Ag. 31, '70. What it would be like if women win. Gloria Steinem.

Time. 98:36-7. Jl. 26, '71. Women's lib: beyond sexual politics. Ruth Brine.

Time. 98:56. Jl. 26, '71. A woman's place is on the job.

Trans-Action. 5:28-30. Ap. '68. Are women prejudiced against women? Philip Goldberg.

Trans-Action. 8:13-80+. N./D. '70. The American woman [special combined issue].

U.S. News & World Report. 67:44-6. S. 8, '69. Woman's changing role in America.

U.S. News & World Report. 67:95-6. N. 17, '69. Working wives: revolution in American family life.

U.S. News & World Report. 69:51-2. Ag. 3, '70. Equal rights for women workers; a new push.

U.S. News & World Report. 69:74-5. N. 16, '70. "Women's lib" in Russia: the myth and the reality.

Vital Speeches of the Day. 36:749-52. O. 1, '70. What's happened to Eve; address, September 10, 1970. Louise Bushnell.

*Wall Street Journal. p 1. Je. 9, '71. Boosting "Liberation": women's studies rise in college popularity. Barbara Isenberg.

*Washington Post. p G 1. Mr. 8, '70. Beneath those charred bras revolution smolders. Mary Wiegers.

Washington Post. p B 1. Mr. 10, '70. Lib sees women's limited roles: "sow to sexpot to sickie." Mary Wiegers.

Washington Post. p B 1. Mr. 11, '70. Women's lib: "only radicals in town." Mary Wiegers.

Washington Post. p G 1. Ap. 26, '70. Women politicians gird for the fight. Marie Smith.

*Woman's Day. p 46-7. My. '71. Raising a bright and happy child. Myrna Blyth.